DAILY MEDITATIONS

Front cover: Pensée sauvage © schnudde|iStock.com

Prosveta S.A – CS30012 – 83601 Fréjus CEDEX (France)

ISBN 978-2-8184-0444-7
original edition: 978-2-8184-0443-0

Omraam Mikhaël Aïvanhov

DAILY MEDITATIONS

2019

P R O S V E T A

Foreword

Every morning, before you do anything else, you must give yourself a few quiet moments of reflection so as to begin your day in peace and harmony, and unite yourself to the Creator by dedicating the new day to Him through prayer, meditation.

It is the beginning that is all-important, for it is then, at the beginning, that new forces are set in motion and given direction. If we want to act wisely and well, we have to begin by casting some light on the situation. You do not look for something or start work in the dark; you start by lighting a lamp so that you can see what you are doing. And you can apply the same principle to every area in life: in order to know what to do and how to do it, you have to switch on the light – in other words, to concentrate and look into yourself. Without this light you will wander in all directions and knock on many different doors, and you will never achieve anything worthwhile.

Our days follow the direction that we give to our first thoughts in the morning, for, depending on whether we are mindful or not, we either clear the way ahead or litter it with all kinds of useless and even dangerous debris. Disciples of initiatic science know how to begin the day so that it may be fruitful and rich in God's grace, and so that they may share that grace with those around them. They understand how important it is to begin the day with one fundamental thought around which all the other thoughts of the day may revolve.

If you keep your sights fixed on a definite goal, a clear orientation, an ideal, all your activities will gradually organize themselves and fall into line in such a way as to contribute to the realization of that ideal. Even the negative or alien thoughts or feelings that attempt to infiltrate you will be deflected and put at the service of the divine world. Yes, even they will be forced to follow the direction you have chosen. In this way, thanks to the fundamental thought that you place in your head and your heart first thing in the morning, your whole day will be recorded in the book of life.

And, since everything we do is recorded, once you have lived one glorious day, one day of eternal life, not only will that day be recorded, not only will it never die, but it will endeavor to get the days that follow to imitate it. Try to live just one day as well as you possibly can, therefore, and it will influence all your days: it will persuade them to listen to its testimony and follow its example, so as to be well balanced, orderly, and harmonious.

Omraam Mikhaël Aïvanhov

Between 1938 and 1985, Omraam Mikhaël Aïvanhov elaborated a spiritual teaching in almost five thousand improvised talks. His words have been preserved in their entirety, as the talks given between 1938 and the early 1960s were taken down in shorthand, and the later ones were recorded on tape and latterly on video.

Many of these recordings have been published in book form by Prosveta, providing a comprehensive guide to the teaching.

GLOSSARY

Definitions of terms as used by the Master Omraam Mikhaël Aïvanhov:

brotherhood: a collectivity governed by a truly cohesive spirit (its members share the common bond of a broad, light-filled consciousness), in which each individual works consciously for the good of all. (Daily Meditations 2007: 24 February)

collectivity [human]: a group of people, usually quite extensive, united by a common interest, a common organization or common sentiments, or living in the same place or country.

collectivity [cosmic]: the totality of beings in the universe, both visible and invisible.

disinterestedness: refers not to a lack of interest but to altruism, an absence of bias motivated by interest or advantage. This is a central part of the Master's philosophy. (A New Dawn, part 2, p. 120)

entities: disincarnate beings, drawn to humans and to nature. They may be either light or dark beings, depending on the quality of the vibrations of the person or place attracting them.

higher self, lower self: must be understood within the context of the Master's teaching concerning the two natures in human beings, the human lower self and the divine higher self, which he calls respectively personality and individuality. (Love and Sexuality, part 2, p. 42)

impersonal: refers not to a coldness of attitude but to the absence of referral to self.

psychic: (adjective – as in 'psychic life / world / bodies, etc.'): refers not to mediumship but to a human being's subtle energy beyond the physical, i.e. heart and mind (and soul, or soul and spirit, according to the context).

spiritualist: refers to anyone who looks at things from a spiritual point of view, whose philosophy of life is based on belief in a spiritual reality. (A New Dawn, part 2, p. 127)

1 January

*T*ry to realize the importance of the moment you awake in the morning, because the rest of your day depends on it and the rest of your life depends on this day. If you do not live the present day correctly, you will spend each tomorrow repairing the consequences of the mistakes you made the previous day. All those who have concerned themselves with the future while neglecting the present twenty-four hours have left gaps everywhere in their life, and they find themselves back on earth to put things right, make amends, and suffer.

By simply living twenty-four hours well, you will prepare the twenty-four hours to come, and the programme that lies ahead will be easier to carry out: the ground has been cleared, nothing lies in the way, so life becomes easy. Therefore start by living the first moments of each day well, in order to prepare the hours that follow. Tell yourself, 'The past is the past, and the future is "yet to come"... but I have today. So, set to work!

2 *January*

Both earth and heaven seek our attention, and we must learn how to work for the one and for the other, first ensuring we make a clear distinction between earthly material values and spiritual values. For as long as we are on earth, abandoning it is out of the question. But we must only place our feet on the ground; we must hold our head in heaven, that is to say, put wisdom and love in everything we do so that everything we undertake brings us closer the divine world.

To illustrate this, I could say that we must see our life on earth akin to plants. Look at trees – they remain fixed to the ground, but thanks to the water and light they receive from above, they transform the earth and foster its evolution by bearing flowers and fruit. Trees show us how we can work on earth while also directing ourselves towards heaven. And this is another lesson nature teaches us: not only must we not neglect earth – matter – we must also endeavour to transform it.

3 January

*L*ove is a science, but very few people care to study it. This is why so many people, when they leave, although filled with good intentions to devote themselves to others and talk about one thing only – love – end up disappointed and bitter after a while. It was inevitable, for it was their unenlightened love that put them in deplorable situations. But then they go about complaining that love is the root of all evils.

In truth, it is people's ignorance about love that creates misfortune, not love itself. Endeavour to connect yourself to God, the Source of eternal life, so that the water in you – your forces, your energies – can continually be renewed. At first, this exercise might seem off-putting: you want to love God, but your heart remains empty, you become bored and let your thoughts wander. But persevere – tell yourself that your whole life depends on this connection you are creating with God. Little by little, you will become so rich and strong that you will be able to help thousands of beings in the world just through the power of thought, for borders are no barrier to thoughts.

4 January

All human beings have a certain physical appearance making them recognizable; certain physical traits simply cannot be mistaken. But, inwardly, they have the faculty to identify themselves with all that exists, and that is exactly what they more or less consciously do throughout each day: through imitation, they continually identify themselves with what they touch, see and hear. As such, we must be vigilant and, from time to time, stop for a moment to ask ourselves with whom or what we are identifying. Because, sooner or later, we will become those beings and things with whom we have fused.

We must above all seek to fuse with the light so that one day, we truly become this light. If we can use the spark within us, our spirit, to gradually illumine our whole being, we will possess the same power and provide the same blessings as the light of the sun.

5 January

What exactly is a dwelling place? It is a place where we shelter, where we work and where we live. But we could say that our physical body itself is a dwelling place, and so too is any body on the physical plane – animals, trees, flowers and stones are all dwelling places.

We have at least two dwelling places on the physical plane: our house and our body. However, dwelling places are not something we have only on the physical plane, they are also present on the psychic and spiritual planes. For on these subtle planes, we also have dwelling places: our astral, mental, causal, buddhic and atmic bodies. And, just as several dwelling places can be housed in the same building, our various psychic dwelling places form part of our physical body.

The notion of a dwelling place goes much further still, for the house made of wood, stone or concrete that shelters our physical body is in turn housed in another much larger and vaster abode: the earth. And the earth dwells in the solar system which itself resides in the cosmos. That is how we can understand the concept of a house.

6 January

*I*t is the role of heavenly beings to fight against evil, not that of humans who don't have the stature, the ability or the methods to do so. All those who imagined they were strong enough to go to war against evil have been brought down, because evil is an extremely powerful cosmic force. However, evil is mistakenly seen as being as powerful as the forces of good, and the devil as an entity strong enough to stand up to God forever. But human beings don't have the capacity to overpower this entity. When some brave people think they have been given the mission to eradicate all the evil in the world, they underestimate the dangers to which they are exposed.

However, this is not a reason to remain inactive until the heavenly entities come to slay what the book of *Revelation* calls the dragon. Every day, while progressing on the path of light, we can strengthen the army of the good, the army of the sons and daughters of God, so as to hasten its victory. When this army is large enough, the entities of darkness will be defeated. If they still exert their destructive activity, it is because humans' greed and inferior desires continue to feed them.

7 January

***T**he heavenly Father and the divine Mother, his Wife, Nature, are our true parents. Those who don't perceive Nature as their divine Mother, cannot have a true connection with their heavenly Father. It is essential for us to realize that above, not only do we have a Father but also a Mother, because our life, just like that of the universe, does not only originate in the expression of the masculine principle, but also in that of the feminine principle.

We have two parents in heaven. We must accept this truth knowing that life will not give in to the ignorance and prejudice of human beings. Because life knows how to protect itself and asks us, 'Why do you seek to maim me by removing one of my two principles that together are the very reason I am life? However, each time I will regain the upper hand.' A religion first and foremost teaches us about life, all life, without discarding or separating anything.

8 January

The first requirement for salvation is vigilance. Never let doubt and confusion take hold of you. At the first sign of threat, instead of becoming dispersed, go higher! Take refuge in your inner sanctum, call on the spirit of God, and ask for advice, for it is he who will give you weapons. Even at the height of the storm, if part of you is able to remain on high, no enemy will be able to harm you. Why is aviation such a formidable weapon in times of war? Because the attacks come from above.

On the spiritual plane, the precautions we must take and the methods we must use are very similar to those used on the physical plane. When an enemy approaches, the forces don't disperse; they band together and go higher. You too must concentrate your forces. And in doing so, you will rise up. Reflect and ask yourself how many times you have been shoved and manhandled for having stayed below in a state of dispersion.

9 January

*W*aiting… disciples of a spiritual teaching learn to cultivate waiting, this inner state that keeps them awake. And so, when beings of light come to visit them, they will be ready to immediately open the doors of their soul to them. This attitude of anticipation alone enables them to perceive the events of the invisible world, the currents that flow through it, and the presences that bring them their blessings. You might say that you have never seen these presences. But is it really necessary to see them? You can feel them, and that is so much more important. If your heart and soul do not feel the revelations heavenly beings bring you, seeing them won't help very much.

If you are waiting to receive a light or blessings from heaven, don't ever be impatient. Instead, learn to cultivate waiting, because at any moment you might receive warning, information, enlightenment, nourishment. For it is thanks to waiting that your subtle centres are always kept awake. In this way, you will develop a kind of sensor that alerts you to the arrival of a messenger, a heavenly visitor.

10 January

*A*ll human beings, whatever their level of evolution, are called upon to progress again and again. If they don't make any effort, it is very often because they imagine the path is closed to them. But it might in fact be open. They must try their hand at various experiences to know what they are capable of. Even if they are not able to go very far, they must keep in mind that divine perfection is the goal of their life on earth. Divine perfection is of course an inaccessible ideal, but they must strive to attain it so as to build their future. They will then be able to master the disparate thoughts, feelings and desires pulling them in all directions and weakening them, and direct them, according to their own intentions, in their pursuit of regeneration.

Every day there is much science to master, discipline to accept, and effort to be made. And that's what is so wonderful: we are in continual movement, making progress and rising upwards. The whole meaning of life is contained in this pursuit of divine perfection.

11 January

*T*he only science worth studying is the science of life. For all the other subjects you touch on, all the other activities you undertake, will only really bring you something if you focus on this one essential reality: life. So, instead of using it to satisfy your desires, ambitions, and whims, learn how to regard life as a goal, and employ all your faculties to reinforce, enlighten and purify it within you, because without life, you have nothing else.

Your intellect, your heart and your will are all nourished by life. When you sustain this life in you, your intellect understands, your heart loves and rejoices, and your will is reinforced and creates. Without life, even knowledge is impossible, and there is no more philosophy, no more religion and no more art. This is why the science of life is the key to all realisations.

12 January

*S*o many people think they are highly intelligent and well informed! When you hear them talk, they have already seen everything, experienced everything, they know everything and they look upon everything around them superficially. This is why they learn almost nothing new and they become blasé. But if they were to try to see everything as if they were seeing it for the first time, not only would they truly learn something new, they would also experience new joys.

When you breathe, you eat and you drink, do so as if for the first time, and everything will appear succulent to you. Act in the same way with the people around you: your husband, your wife, your children, and your friends. You might say that it will require a large amount of auto-suggestion to rediscover someone in whom you have already lost interest. That is true, but if you persevere, if you really search, this ability for suggestion will enable you to discover another reality.

13 January

*L*ife is perpetual movement. This is why human beings must always be in motion and always look ahead. Those who refuse to move forward regress. They lose the memory of the divine imprint engraved in them and return to the unconscious state of stone which is nothing but sleeping consciousness. Despite their human appearance, so many people are, like stones, incapable of getting themselves moving – they have to be continually pushed to get them to shift. They should at least make the effort to leave the mineral kingdom to become plants and grow. Later, like animals, they will learn to move.

It is a great ability to be able to look for food, to escape danger, and take cover from bad weather without outside intervention. The day humans develop the same capacities on the psychic plane, they will make great progress. But they have yet to truly reach the human kingdom, that is to say the world of spirit, in order to become masters of their destiny.

14 January

H*umans too often seek nourishment in what is not essential. They spend the good part of their time in occupations which bring nothing to their spirit, and they justify themselves by claiming that their daily life, their responsibilities, their family, their work, and society force them into activities in which the spirit cannot partake. This is not true, for the spirit can have its say anywhere.

In order to always keep sight of what is essential, we must organize our life around this centre, the spirit, the spark which lives within us. As such, all our activities and even our distractions will contribute to nourishing life in us. The spirit dwelling in humans does not reject their liver, their intestines or their feet under the pretext that their work is not as noble. Everything has its own place and serves the spirit. But the moment this unifying and governing force is missing from the centre, all the elements start to disperse, and death – spiritual death – ensues.

15 January

*I*n order to stay on the right path, carefully study the inner relationships between your lower nature and your higher nature. When you make good resolutions – for example, if you want to get rid of a bad habit or want to help someone – know that your lower nature watches you and will send you suggestions and temptations to try to distract you from your good intentions. Or it might wait patiently to take its revenge. Humans' lower nature is inhabited by an entire population which, like all populations on earth, does not only constitute honest, noble and generous beings, but also evil entities seeking to impose themselves there too.

When your higher nature makes plans, if you want to bring them to fruition, seize the moments when your lower nature has dozed off, for otherwise it will rise up and do everything in its power to take over. It will whisper to you, 'There's no rush. You have all the time you need. Why go to all this trouble when you could just take it easy?' There are specific precautions you need to take so as not to be tempted to abandon your good intentions.

16 January

*T*hose who persist in describing hell as a place where miserable sinners are doomed to eternal punishment do not realize how this belief contradicts the love of God, for God never rejects anyone forever. This belief also goes against God's wisdom, because God, who is wise, never lets anything go to waste – in his creation, everything can be used and everything is put to use.

This is another area to explore: the laws of the cosmic economy. As on the physical plane, the same is true on the psychic plane where unclean elements are sent to a place where they are transformed by certain entities. There is a whole system of pipes from which the purified matter emerges to then travel along other circuits to feed, water and fertilize other unknown regions. It is not always the same impure elements that accumulate and stagnate in hell, for new waste constantly arrives to replace what has already been transformed. As such, we can say that hell is a place cut off from divine light, but renewed materials emerge from it to re-enter the stream of life.

17 January

*W*e don't always possess the right criteria to identify those who are proud and those who are humble. People who are obedient and submissive are seen as humble and are appreciated: they don't disturb others or stand up to them. But is this really a virtue? No, because often, this humility is not inspired by wisdom and real understanding, but rather by fear, weakness and ignorance.

People without money, social rank, the virtues or the abilities enabling them to assert themselves cannot achieve much. But if they were given such capacities, would they still be humble? Nothing is less certain. We cannot judge people before we come to know them and observe them.

18 January

*T*he physical appearances of people who have lived on earth are recorded in the cosmic archives. In spiritualist meetings, when someone who lived in the distant past is mentioned, even if they have reincarnated several times since then, they manifest through the medium and speak in exactly the same way as they did in the past. In reality, they themselves are not actually present, it is only their appearance, one that can be seen and almost touched.

Every human being that incarnates on earth receives an appearance which they leave behind at the end of their life – it is used for one incarnation only and is kept in the universe's archives. When humans incarnate again, they receive another appearance and it too will be recorded. There will always be new appearances and they will all be recorded until the day the universe ceases to exist.

19 January

Artists who painted angels, archangels and divinities, often depicted them in magnificent clothes and adorned with gold and precious stones. They intuitively knew there was a correspondence between spiritual wealth and material wealth. The tradition of vestments adorned with precious stones, still present to this day, has the same meaning: an officiating priest's spiritual wealth must be shown by the external wealth of their clothing.

And if you too wear jewellery adorned with precious stones, know that you must also possess these stones within you: sapphires symbolize peace; rubies, love; amethysts, sacrifice; the topaz, wisdom; emeralds, hope; diamonds, strength of spirit. There is endless wealth in the symbolism of precious stones and their full potential is yet unknown.

20 January

Spiritual life is a long walk towards a promised land that is first and foremost within us, and we must set off again each day to draw closer to it. Just like nomads in the desert continually search for wells and oases, we must constantly keep moving.

So many spiritualists believe that they will find the Promised Land while staying in the same place. They shut themselves up inside themselves – symbolically speaking in a house with thick walls – and not only do they remain inside, but they amass countless useless and cumbersome objects. They would do better to leave this house behind and take only what is necessary for their journey. In order to reach the Promised Land, all they need is a small tent and to cultivate sobriety by seeking food for their soul and spirit.

21 January

*W*hy is it that so many members of the clergy depict God as a ruthless judge who punishes humans for the slightest transgression they make? In reality, God does not administer punishment, but the universe he created is based on laws, and these laws also govern human beings and their physical life, as well as their psychic and spiritual life. It is these laws that are strict, and those who do not respect them expose themselves to punishment. And as a result, this punishment may even spread down to their children.

Take a well-known example – that of alcoholism. Alcohol abuse is detrimental not only to the physical and mental health of those who overindulge, but also to that of their children. The same is true for all other kinds of overindulgence and transgression. This is how divine Justice manifests in order to make humans aware of their responsibilities.

22 *January*

*O*ne way or another, every problem we have to solve in life and each of our decisions and experiences brings up the question of what we must sacrifice in order to live a rich and beautiful life.

But most humans, not having understood what sacrifice is, see it as deprivation and loss, and there are indeed unnecessary sacrifices which can thus be seen as losses. Know that making sacrifices, in the spiritual sense of the word, is not about sacrificing yourself, but to let something useless or harmful die within you, in order to receive something great, powerful and precious in return. If you do not sacrifice something inferior in you in favour of fostering something superior, you will no doubt sacrifice what is best in you to the benefit of the most unrefined instincts. It is impossible to escape this law that dictates that your higher nature can only live if you sacrifice your lower nature in favour of it. What life is for one means death for the other. True sacrifice is to give up your limited, weak and poor self so as to live in your divine self.

23 *January*

Christian tradition, following on from Jewish tradition, teaches the existence of nine angelic orders. From the bottom up, these are the angels, the archangels, the principalities, the virtues, the powers, the dominions, the thrones, the Cherubim, and the Seraphim. The Cabbalah names them *kerubim*, *bnei-elohim*, *elohim*, *malakhim*, *seraphim*, *hashmalim*, *aralim*, *ophanim*, and *hayoth hakadesch*. Each of these angelic orders is an aspect of divine power and virtues. Even if we cannot picture them, it is easier to create an idea of them and to relate to the divine world if we pronounce their names rather than simply pronouncing the word 'God'.

It is important for your spiritual development to know that these angelic hierarchies exist, for they are like beacons along your path to the summit. Try to familiarize yourself with them and invoke them in order to rise up in prayer and meditation to the throne of God. Then, think that through them you bring the blessings of heaven down to earth.

24 *January*

*A*mong the four elements, it is not earth but water that corresponds best to the way we can understand matter. Water is the symbol of primordial matter that received the fertilizing seeds of spirit, and this is why, in the beginning of the book of *Genesis*, we are told that *'a wind from God swept over the face of the waters'*. Water is the matrix of life. Life emerged from water thanks to the principle of fire – spirit – that put water in motion. Without the action of fire, life is not possible. Alone, water – matter – has no life; it is fire that infused life in it.

On earth, our planet, life is also born of the action of fire on water. The first seeds of life, brought by the sun's rays, travelled to the ocean's waters that welcomed them like a loving mother. She carried them in her womb and they grew, multiplied and gave rise to all the forms of life that we know today.

25 *January*

If humans have no real criteria with which to analyze the motives for their expectations and demands, the political arena will remain a place of confrontation. Just how many times throughout history have there been revolutions and changes in regime! But regardless of the intended reforms, there can be no real progress until there is a change in consciousness and mentality.

Only when humans choose to abandon the narrow confines of their selfish appetites will the changes they propose bring real improvements. Until then, we will continue to see the same relentless efforts of a few ambitious and greedy people vying fiercely for the positions that will bring them more power and money. But how many of them truly prepare themselves for the great task that really lies before them? And as for those who elect them, do they not do so in the hope to in turn satisfy their own greed?

26 January

*N*o gesture remains totally ineffective. Every gesture is magical by nature: it produces currents, colours and vibrations that reach beings in space. Each gesture opens or closes certain doors to us and puts us in contact with harmful or favourable forces. So what are we to think about all these hysterical gesticulations that are now called dancing? How can we make these ignorant people understand that each movement is like a pebble thrown into the ocean of energies, creating waves that necessarily one day return to their point of origin, and that if they take a knock it should come as no surprise to them.

We can also compare the gestures we make to letters that we constantly address to the visible and invisible worlds. They are secret signs we can use to make contact with all reasonable or unreasonable beings of nature. They are expressions of our intellect and our heart, and through them we either create our future or destroy it.

27 *January*

*W*hen you succeed in creating a state of inner silence, peace and light, you are able to reach, for a moment at least, the regions of your soul and spirit that you have carried within you since the very beginning. Most human beings are not even aware of these regions that are so difficult to attain in everyday life. For, just as they are unaware of what goes on in their subconscious, they are also oblivious to what goes on up on high, in heaven, in their spirit, and in their divine consciousness.

For example, when you meditate on a spiritual question that you find difficult to solve, you go deep within yourself to seek an answer. After some time, enlightenment gradually emerges from this silence, and you receive an answer. What happened? Where does this comprehension come from? Your spirit knew the answer, but your consciousness was not yet able to rise up that far. But now, far from the hustle and bustle, your thoughts can soar into space and you receive a revelation.

28 January

*W*hy is it that so many people are dull, cold, stiff and tense? No warmth or light emanates from them. They will tell you they like poetry, but they leave it to the poets who write it. From time to time, they read a few verses, but the life they themselves lead is not poetic, and this is why they have so little joy in meeting each other. When will they understand that true art, the art of the future, is to make life poetical by becoming more expressive and alive themselves, and by cultivating their own warmth and light?

Humans are extraordinary: they expect others to bring them comfort, friendship, love and light, but they themselves remain passive, uncommunicative, dull and prosaic. This poetical life for which others love them remains elusive to them. Each day, they must endeavour to spread light and heat so as to go beyond themselves and their mundane apathy. It is so very pleasant to meet a poet – a being in whom you sense that everything is alive, vivid and enlightened!

29 January

Hypnosis acts on a person's subconscious by immersing them in a state similar to sleep. Once in this kind of trance, they carry out the orders they are given – something they may not do in a conscious state. We can also infer that by placing an image of our desire in our subconscious, we will be able to achieve that desire more quickly.

Here is a method that will help you in your spiritual work. If you would like to cultivate a specific quality or virtue, just before falling asleep start by focusing on this quality and meditate on the goal you want to achieve with it: during your sleep, the power of your subconscious will help materialize your desire. If I so often insist on the importance of the state in which you fall asleep every night, it is because sleep favours the crystallization of all your inner states. You must learn to fall asleep with the best thoughts and desires, because this helps manifest them.

30 January

*S*o many books have been written to reveal God's law to humans! But before being inscribed in books, this law was first etched in their hearts. However, every religion is presented as a set of beliefs and doctrines it seeks to impose on its followers. And not only must they accept them, they are also expected to believe that their religion is superior to all others and that it is the only one that will bring them salvation. But this is only fanaticism.

It would of course not be reasonable to leave humans to their own devices on the pretext they must read God's law in their hearts, for most of them are not yet ready. For them to be able to read this law correctly, they must be taught to bring order to their inner world and to master their thoughts and desires, otherwise what they read within themselves will be no more than the product of their imagination or even of their most primitive instincts. The duty of religions is first and foremost to teach humans how to read the law God etched inside of them.

31 January

*T*hose who are truly great accept to serve others to help them to see more clearly and to find the best solutions to their problems, even if these problems seem insignificant to them. Spiritual Masters and the wise do not fear lowering themselves to the level of those who are small, weak and ignorant, for they know that in doing so, they will not descend from the summit they have reached within themselves. They never use their superiority to dominate others. They know that the higher they have risen, the more humility they must show. Having superior moral and spiritual virtues is all well and good, but it does not suffice. For the next question is that of their attitude and behaviour. No knowledge or spiritual power gives them the right to dominate others and to impose themselves on them.

May each person rise as high as they can, but only within themselves; on the outside they must not put themselves up on a pedestal. There is no sense in elevating themselves if it is to later trample their fellow human beings. Initiates and the wise know how to manifest their greatness through love, kindness and gentleness.

1 February

*T*he cold is often seen in a negative light and is equated with contraction and paralysis; while heat symbolizes something alive and generous. In reality, there are two types of heat and cold. There is heat which dilates and brings life and maturity, and heat which burns and dries. There is the cold that preserves all that is good, and cold that paralyzes life.

Take for example the water cycle in nature. When exposed to the heat of the sun's rays, water heats up and evaporates. Once in the upper atmosphere, it cools down, crystallizes and falls back to the earth in the form of snow. When the sun melts the snow, water runs down into the valleys where it joins the rivers, the lakes and the oceans. It then evaporates and the cycle starts over again. This is how nature uses the alternation of heat and cold to sustain life.

As for humans, their intellect must be cold so they may think correctly and progress on the path of wisdom; while their heart must remain warm to express love.

2 February

Humans naturally tend to rank things, whether it is intelligence, talent, strength, dexterity, beauty, wealth and so on. Everywhere, something always comes first and something else comes last. But these ratings are very relative. When considering a limited number of individuals, we can talk about someone being first and someone else being last; but when considering life as an endless and unbroken chain, how can we identify what comes first and what comes last? Similarly, if we were to compare life to a turning wheel, the first position becomes the last position and vice versa.

And who comes first in a family: the father, the mother or the child? In terms of age, the child comes last, but in terms of importance it comes first because their father and mother dedicate their full attention to it. Or take for example those who come first when it comes to being wise, smart or educated: they come last when it comes to physical strength, and vice versa. This is the nature of things – those who come first in one area come last in another. So you can all be happy knowing that you come first in some domain or another.

3 February

*T*he Christ is a cosmic principle, a principle that can manifest in those who are prepared to receive it. But humans, however exceptional they may be, cannot be Christ, they cannot be the incarnation of God himself. The Christ has never taken a physical body, will never do so, and is unable to become a human being. The Christ only enters the souls and spirits ready to receive it and become one with it. This is how the Christ merged with all the great spiritual Masters we know of in humanity, and also with many others that we don't know.

Christ remains a spirit. And Jesus, like all the other initiates, had a long road to travel before the spirit of Christ descended into him. If he was called Jesus Christ, it is not because he was Christ, but because he received the Christ. And if he received the Christ, it was because he had the highest consciousness of God's presence within him. It is therefore this consciousness that humans must develop until they melt into the Divine so they can one day say, like Jesus, 'The Father and I are one'.

4 February

Words of truth can only be understood and above all, put into action, if they fall on fertile ground. To better understand this, we must first bear in mind the psychic structure of human beings. It is based on three principles: an intellect which allows us to think, a heart enabling us to express feelings, and a will encouraging us to take action. But our will never acts without motive – it is influenced by our thoughts and feelings.

Observe yourselves when you wish to take action: it is not enough to simply think something is useful for you to decide to do it; you also need to like what you are going to do. We can therefore say that actions are the materialization of thoughts produced by the intellect and of feelings inspired by the heart – actions are their children. And depending on the quality of these thoughts and feelings, the actions our will produces will be good or bad. They are good if our intellect is inspired by wisdom and our heart inspired by love. Only then can we act according to the truth: for truth manifests through will, like a seed that grows in fertile soil.

5 February

*W*hat do we really know about human beings? We can describe their physical body and touch them, but it is impossible to describe or touch the entity that formed their body or that dwells within them and gives them life. Think of someone's body lying on the ground, they are visible and you can touch them, but they are dead: something invisible has left them – that 'something' that made them walk, talk, love and think. You can place beside them all the food and treasures in the world and say, 'This is for you, all of it, my old friend, enjoy it!' That will not change anything, they won't budge.

At first sight, the world around us – the world that we can see, touch and measure – appears to be the only reality there is. But although it is real, it is not the whole reality. It is only the concrete and material manifestation of an invisible world of forces, currents and entities. Our five senses do not give us access to the true reality.

6 February

Holiness, contrary to what many people think, does not mean a man and a woman must avoid feeling attracted to one another. Holiness is not achieved by refraining from love, because love is life, and holiness requires life. But just as there are varying degrees of life, the same is true of love.

Love, true love, is not only beyond sexual attraction, it is even beyond feelings. It is a higher state of consciousness. There are certain virtues that help us draw closer to this true knowledge of love, and among them, the most important is purity. And when I speak of purity, I mean purity of thoughts and feelings: thoughts and feelings free of self-centredness. The three words 'life', 'love' and 'purity' are connected, because life depends on love, and the purer love is, the more rich, good and luminous life is.

7 February

Human beings will always be inhabited by instincts and desires, the reasons for their downfall. But they must not seek to fight or to root out these instincts and desires, for they are the roots of their being, and if they tear up their roots, the source of their life will eventually dry up. They must only strive to transform and purify these instincts and desires. However, everywhere today, words such as 'tear up' and 'root out' are more easily understood than words like 'transform', 'transmute', and 'purify'. There is therefore much work to be done in this regard.

When you feel a desire might make you act in a bad way, it is often useless to try and ward it off. Don't confront it head on. Instead, seek to rise up to the plane of feelings and thought, of soul and spirit, and then orient this desire in different way. Every day we must endeavour to purify and ennoble our desires because through their either dark or luminous nature, we connect with corresponding entities and regions in space.

8 February

*T*oo many faithful see God as addressing humans to dictate his will: 'Go here, do this and that.' No, God does not express himself like that and does not give orders. You might say, 'But does he never speak to us? Does he never tell us what to do?' Of course he speaks to us, every moment of every day. He tells us, 'Be firm in wisdom, love and truth'. And then it's up to us to find when, where and how we can best manifest these three virtues.

But many people, instead of hearing this voice encouraging them to work patiently and to perfect themselves, convince themselves that God has given them the mission to convert the infidels, and even to massacre them if they resist. No, such ignorant people will become monsters. They must know that they have no power over the souls of others, and it is they themselves who are losing their soul.

9 February

*M*any people, feeling far superior to others, spend their time criticizing them and feel satisfied and take pride in doing so. In reality, this is actually a weakness of which they must not be proud. Every negative word feeds dark entities that use it for carrying out their evil designs. You might say that people don't always really think the negative things they say about others. That may be so, but they nevertheless gave the dark entities the means with which to inflict harm.

Avoid criticism, especially if you are not completely sure about the facts you describe. And even if, for some or other reason, you must speak about the incorrect behaviour of someone, for instructive reasons, try to conclude by mentioning at least one of their good qualities. Highlighting the faults or the bad behaviour of others has never improved them. Criticism only fuels evil.

10 February

*I*n one of his aspects, God appears as Mother nature who sets boundaries her children must not cross. If they do cross them, it is said that God punishes them. This is not so, for they are the ones who left the enclosure sheltering and protecting them, and in so doing they put themselves in danger.

Humans must stop thinking that the acts they commit are foreign to them, and that once they have done something, they are free of it. No, whether it be good or bad deeds, even if they escape human justice, their errors will leave indelible traces behind within them. If they wish to experience divine love and kindness, there is only thing to do: they must not err; and if they do, they must realize their mistakes and make amends.

11 February

When birds see danger approaching, they fly away. You should do the same: when you feel threatened, fly away and rise up so high that, at least within yourselves, you will be safe from all forms of aggression. This is the advice wisdom gives. But if humans find it so difficult to follow, it is because they tend to obey the law of action and reaction. When they are hurt, they retaliate and take revenge, and often even doubly so. Problems cannot be solved this way.

When you see the way some people act, you wonder if they really want to solve the problem and find ways to live in harmony. You might even say they find confronting others amusing over time: they test their strength, they score points or they lose some, and then try to score some more. This fight tires them out, but they find that natural. Natural for them maybe, but not in the eyes of divine wisdom that advises us to settle conflicts by rising on high.

12 February

A child's father and mother are like building contractors that have been commissioned to build a house for a soul. They are responsible only for the construction of this house and the materials used to build it – they have no power over the child's soul itself: they don't know where it comes from and it will also leave without them knowing when or where.

The loss of a child is a terrible ordeal for parents, I know, and many have come to me seeking advice and comfort. Rebellion does not change anything and can even increase their suffering. If they were good, loving and attentive parents, they will leave magnificent imprints on their child. Their child's soul, having left, will be eternally grateful and will never forget them. It will come from the invisible world to comfort them and bring them presents of tenderness and light, and continue to live beside them.

13 February

*I*f you remain on the astral plane, the region of feelings and emotions, you will never find the inner stability and security you seek. In this region, the climate and the weather conditions constantly change: one moment the sun is shining and you are happy; the next, it is cloudy and you become sad. One moment you love, and moments later something happens and you don't love anymore. And the mental plane, the world of thought, is no more stable: just how often do you change your mind based on events or what you believe to be of interest to you. You can only encounter disappointment and make mistakes.

To move on solid and stable ground, you must change planes, that is to say, leave the astral and mental planes – the feelings and thoughts of your lower nature – and rise up to the causal plane. Since you will always have a heart and intellect – feelings and thoughts – you will always have something to do on the astral and mental planes. But you must set up your home on the floor above – on the causal plane. For that is where you will receive the light for you to face all situations.

14 February

*T*he words of Jesus, *'I am the way, the truth and the life'* are written in many churches and temples. To understand their meaning, we must understand the three words 'way', 'truth' and 'life' in relation to each other. And at first this seems almost impossible. But an image, that of a river, can help us. A river originates at a source where water flows fourth. This source represents the truth. The water, life, flows and over time it digs its bed and creates its path.

In the beginning, there is always a source – the truth. Water – life flowing from this source – is love. And the bed of the river – the way – is wisdom. As the water flows from the source, it flows down bringing life to the entire universe. If we wish to drink this water in its purest form, we must retrace the river up to the source by following the path of wisdom. Fed by love that is life, and guided by wisdom, the way, we reach the source, the truth.

15 February

***H**uman beings are composed of matter, the physical body, and of a subtle principle, the spirit. But above all, human beings are spirits. If they have been given bodies, it is so that through them, the spirit can manifest and work on the physical plane.

The relation of human beings' bodies to their spirit is what the universe is to God's spirit. The universe is God's body, and through this body, his spirit reveals all its riches. The universe only exists because God's spirit continues to penetrate it in order to animate it and give it life. If God withdrew, the universe would return to nothingness. And the same is true for humans: when the spirit animating them leaves their body, it takes with it all its treasures: life, energy and consciousness, and their body disintegrates.

16 February

For centuries, the Church has taught Christians that the original sin of Adam and Eve has left something impure in human beings and that it is carried down from one generation to the next, with nothing for them to cleanse themselves of it: they are conceived in sin and born in sin, and it is impossible to avoid this fatality. Well, it is precisely by insisting on this idea and promulgating it to such a degree, that the Church prevents humanity from righting itself, for it lessens peoples' hope and desire to extricate themselves from their weak and limited situation.

Of course, there is some degree of truth in the fact that humans are conceived in sin, because their parents and all those who went before pass on to them an already defective inheritance thanks to their unenlightened and impure behaviour, thoughts and feelings. But as for the idea that, ever since Adam and Eve, original sin is inevitably passed on from one generation to the next – no. If humans find the light and seek to live in this light, the sin of Adam and Eve no longer matters.

17 February

***H**uman beings keep saying that 'the flesh is weak' in order to justify not being able to resist temptation. But in fact, the flesh, our body, is neutral: it is just the intermediary through which we can realize our thoughts, feelings and desires. Not only does it not oblige us to make mistakes or go to extremes, but thanks to it we can undertake magnificent work; in fact, it is the best instrument we have for our evolution. Cosmic Intelligence has placed inside us all the instruments we need in order to vibrate in unison with heavenly order and harmony.

There are temples, churches and cathedrals, places that have been consecrated as dwelling places of the Divine. But no sacred building can be compared to a purified, enlightened, and sanctified human body. It is this body that must become a temple. But how much time will it take for humans to accept at least this idea? By continually placing their bodies in the service of their own desires, they turn it into a den of animals, and then it is obviously not the Lord who will come to dwell there, but inferior and undesirable entities who really appreciate this company.

18 February

Stability is the virtue on which we must base our inner life. But what is stability? Someone who is stable is someone who, having decided to walk the path of the light, maintains their divine direction no matter what. As soon as they understand a truth and accept it in their heart and soul, not only do they never allow it to fade in them, they also make it a rule for life, a programme to follow. Stability is a very rare quality. The greatest difficulty for those who have embraced spiritual life is not so much reaching a higher level of consciousness, but maintaining it. One day they are victorious, but the next, the external or internal conditions having changed, they are more negligent, and tend to take another direction and get lost.

In reality, keeping course permanently without flinching on high is almost impossible. This is why stability is the ultimate goal of initiation, when a disciple can finally say, just like the hierophant in ancient Egypt, 'I am stable, the child of stable, conceived and begotten in the land of stability.'

19 February

*T*he feminine principle possesses the keys to realization in matter. It is this principle that materializes, whether it be good or evil. It is indeed the role of women to bring children into the world, but children can also be the symbol of any accomplishment on the psychic and spiritual planes. The same laws apply on whatever plane – physical, psychological or spiritual.

Women are formed in such a way that very subtle particles or etheric matter emanate from them, and this matter can be used to embody ideas and projects, or give them a body. As such, all women must be aware of their powers and decide what projects they wish to associate themselves with. The salvation of humanity depends on the direction women will take. Just like the plane of archetypes where there is only one Woman at the top, the divine Mother, all women on earth should unite to form one woman, the collective woman who will give birth to the new life. The new life will come thanks to women, all women, because they possess the matter in which this new life can manifest.

20 February

When you read a book, listen to music, or contemplate a painting or the marvels of nature, you may suddenly feel you grasped a truth that transforms your way of seeing things. This revelation can last until the next day, the day after, and even much longer, because through this book, music, painting or these sights of nature, your spirit rose on high and grasped meaning. It is like an element of eternity that entered you.

Of course, occasionally having a moment of inspiration, receiving light or giving meaning to your life does not suffice; you must learn to make this moment last for it to become a permanent state of consciousness that purifies, brings order and restores everything in you. Even if it is impossible to escape the hardships and torments in everyday life, it is possible to maintain this meaning within you, and even use the difficulties and torments you face to strengthen it.

21 February

***H**uman beings' intellect is naturally inhabited by pride, and their heart is naturally quick to react with anger. Pride and anger are two violent poisons that are difficult to neutralize, and yet their antidotes do exist. The antidote to pride is humility, and the antidote to anger is gentleness.

Gentleness and humility are two virtues that make it possible to find solutions to the most difficult situations. Contrary to what many people tend to believe, those who know how to manifest these virtues are not weak. For those with a heart warmed by their soul and an intellect enlightened by their spirit, walk on the path of power. People who believe that cultivating humility and gentleness will necessarily make them slaves or victims are wrong; instead, they accumulate a supply of power that enables them to better defend themselves and gain the upper hand in the name of good.

22 *February*

When we see the state of the world today, we tell ourselves the worst may yet happen: nuclear war, epidemics, famines, natural disasters, and so on, capable of bringing an end to humankind. But events are never absolutely certain, for they can take quite a different course, depending on human beings' behaviour.

Nothing is predetermined and there is no fixed destiny, whether it be for an individual or for the world as a whole. When God created humans, he gave them free will, and they determine their own future. If they live without awareness and lead a dissolute life, they unleash chaotic currents and then of course, the laws of nature, which are the laws of justice, will lead them to their loss; it is purely mathematical. But if they think about the consequences of their actions, if they make wise decisions, if they radiate harmonious energy and no longer disturb the balance of nature, many tragedies will be avoided.

23 February

*H*uman beings' true strength does not lie in their ability to harden themselves to avoid suffering while enduring hardships. Their true strength is the ability to accept suffering with clarity and selflessness, and above all with the peace and unity of the spirit.

When people suffer great hardships, the worst experience for them is to feel abandoned by everyone. And each one of us may experience this at least once in our life. But this feeling of abandonment, as painful as it may be, is necessary – it compels people to progress on the spiritual path. If they live the easy life and are satisfied and surrounded by friends, they cannot rise up to the truths of their soul and spirit; for them to discover what is essential, they must be obliged to do so, and experience solitude and lack of support. In reality, no being is abandoned in the true sense of the word. Even when we have to go through the most terrible ordeals, we are surrounded by beings of light that speak to us and watch over us. Loneliness does not exist, it is only a transient state of consciousness, and for us to go beyond this state of consciousness as quickly as possible, we must never doubt the Being who sustains all worlds.

24 February

*I*n nature, all creatures serve as food for others. This is a law, and this law is true on the psychic plane just as it is on the physical plane. What exactly is the battle between good and evil? It is the clash of two hungry entities. It's very obvious – all they do is devour each other.

In humans, good and evil are present in the form of their higher nature and their lower nature. The greatest desire of the lower nature is to grab us and devour us. It tries to catch us and feed off us twenty times, thirty times, fifty times a day. And those who were not vigilant sacrifice a few morsels to their lower nature. They then feel weakened, while their still famished lower nature sets off in search of new prey. This is why we must put our higher nature first and, each day, make sure it can get its teeth on a few pieces of our lower nature. After chewing it well and swallowing it, our higher nature transforms it and makes it its own. Psychology of the future will be based on the understanding of this process: absorption, digestion and assimilation of our lower nature by our higher nature.

25 February

We often hear certain well-known scientists express indignation because humans have not yet rid themselves of what they call irrational beliefs. And even more so since they must admit that after a period of materialism and scientism, more and more people are once again turning to religion, spirituality or mysticism. And this tendency sometimes takes completely confused, nonsensical or insane forms, like fanaticism. Religious authorities of course find this disturbing and feel totally overwhelmed by these new trends they are unable to control. But they are responsible for this situation: for so long they were more preoccupied with spreading the domination of their community, their 'chapel', than with responding to the real needs of souls and spirits. The responsibility also lies with scientists and the limitations of their materialistic philosophy.

Rather than complaining or getting angry about a situation they themselves played a part in creating, both groups should instead come together and see how they can change it.

26 February

*I*magine someone who knows absolutely nothing about the anatomy or physiology of the human body: they might wonder how everything comes together to create a being who walks, breathes, eats, and expresses thoughts and feelings. They would need to be shown that under the skin they see, there is flesh, organs, muscles, blood vessels, nerves, and so on that they cannot see and, finally, a skeleton to hold everything together.

Well, the same is true for the universe, but on a colossal scale. The universe is a body, the body of God, and our physical body is created in its image. Just as our body has a framework, a skeleton, without which it would collapse, so too is the universe supported by a structure which holds everything in equilibrium, from the galaxies to the most infinitesimal particles of matter forming atoms. It is this structure that makes life possible and it constitutes what initiatic philosophy calls the world of principles.

27 February

A summit is not only a point that is higher than others. Every summit, of whatever nature, is a living centre of pure energies. Such a summit also exists in all human beings: their spirit. This is why when they pray for help, they must first seek to reach this summit within themselves. And once they have reached it, they contact the centre of energies governing everything.

You may say there is a huge, even insurmountable distance separating you from this summit within you, your spirit. Of course, but you are able to reach it through thought. Thought is like a rope that you thrust up towards this point on high that you wish to reach. And even if this summit is still far away, at least you are 'tied on' and unlikely to fall.

28 February

*E*xterminating creatures is contrary to divine wisdom, even if they are evil. But so too is leaving them dormant. According to Cosmic Intelligence there must be neither death nor inactivity; it wants to see life and activity manifested everywhere. This is why it anticipates that the infernal creatures that form the egregor religions call Satan, or the devil, can also be educated and one day return to God. The Lord waits for them, his patience is infinite and he is not in a hurry.

How do I know that? Because quite simply, I read it. Where did I read it? Not in the books of human beings, but in the book of living nature. In this book I discovered that the life of God, the love of God descends into the depths and the abysses of the earth. Even there, a few particles of divine life still remain that enable the inhabitants of these regions to survive. And since the life of God descends into the depths, it means that the creatures of the deep can also benefit from it and redeem themselves.

1 March

For countries that manufacture arms, nothing is obviously more profitable than exporting them. And that's how they are able to sell all kinds of increasingly deadly weapons to nations who could jeopardize the peace and security of the entire planet with their endless conflicts. Regardless of whether some people hardly know how to read or write, the most sophisticated weapons are delivered to them, and experts are sent to train them in their use. On one hand, a lot of money is made; but on the other, such profit will prove to be very costly. So much is spent trying to put an end to conflicts that break out all over the world!

We must therefore also understand economics as the science of making forecasts. For a good economist, the immediate advantages do not suffice – what will happen later? And the day people realize that that they have set out on a dangerous path, it is very difficult to turn back.

2 March

*T*he purpose of spiritual life is to give birth to the divine principle in our soul. But to give birth to this child, everyone must be both man and woman, father and mother. As a father, they trigger the process of conception, and as a mother, that of instruction: they guide their child and nourish it. Genuine spiritualists are therefore beings of fullness: the masculine principle and the feminine principle live in perfect harmony in them, and this harmony makes them creators.

From the spiritual point of view, whether they be men or women, married or not, all human beings who are unable to achieve this harmonious union of the masculine principle and the feminine principle in them are considered as single. Unlike what happens on the physical plane, those who are spiritually single cannot bear children. Every manifestation in life is a form of birth. On the spiritual plane, a child can only be born from the union of the soul (the higher heart) and the spirit (the higher intellect).

3 March

***L**ife only has meaning to those who place themselves in service of a great idea: beauty, peace, justice, brotherhood, and so on. An idea is a living being that works on them: it shapes them and models them to the point that one day, they come to embody something of this world of perfection in their way of thinking and acting.

An idea – a living being – is endowed with specific qualities. So, the moment you work for it, you benefit from its wealth. Even if you have only one idea, despite all your weak points, this idea that lives in the kingdom of light puts you in contact with all its friends and introduces you to other beings and other regions on high. We must understand the magical nature of the concept of an idea because what is true of the power of ideas inspired by good is also true of the power of ideas inspired by evil. That is why you must be lucid and vigilant before accepting an idea and deciding to implement it.

4 March

*T*hanks to certain texts you read or people you meet, you begin to discover the wealth of spiritual life. It is only natural to feel the need to share your discovery with others. Yet, try to be careful and reserved. For you must work for a long time to strengthen your convictions and aspirations. If you start to tell others that you have finally found the path of light and that you are determined to follow it and so on, you will set up obstacles for yourself and provoke responses. It is better not to reveal your aspirations until they have begun to materialize. Look after them out of sight and nurture them with your best thoughts and feelings.

A house has doors and windows, and just as it is useful to be able to open them, it is also useful to be able to close them. When we close them, it is generally to protect us from the cold and from noise, dust, or intruders. In spiritual life too, you must know how to close certain doors and windows to protect yourselves.

5 March

If it is so difficult to define truth, it is because it does not exist as such: only wisdom and love exist. It is human beings' behaviour that reveals whether they live in the truth, not the theories they present to others. As for those who claim to seek the truth but have not found it, they must understand that there is actually nothing to look for: all they have to do is progress in love and wisdom each day of their life.

Love and wisdom lead to truth. Truth cannot be conceived of independantly of the heart and intellect. If it did not depend on the activity of the heart and the intellect, everyone would discover the same truth. This however is not the case – everyone, or almost everyone, finds a different truth. Only those who possess love and wisdom discover the same truth. That is why they basically speak the same language despite their different origins and cultures.

6 March

*H*umans are rarely concerned with what is happening in their solar plexus even when they feel discomfort. That shows their lack of knowledge, because even if the solar plexus is a centre that is part of the sympathetic nervous system and thus belongs to their physical body, it plays an important role in their psychic life and even in their spiritual life. That is why you must avoid all states causing tension in the solar plexus or causing it to lose energy: anxiety, anger, fear, nervousness, and all disharmonious and violent feelings. And if it can tighten up and empty, the solar plexus can also expand and fill up. Among the various possible methods, the easiest is to take a hot foot bath. It does not have to last very long. The most important is to take it consciously, and gently touch your feet while focusing on your solar plexus.

The solar plexus can even become a guide for those who learn how to work with it: it communicates information about people, objects and events almost instantaneously. We sometimes talk about a sixth sense. The solar plexus is already a form of sixth sense.

7 March

For thousands of years, Cosmic Intelligence has installed in humans an entire network of subtle channels through which sexual energy, by taking the path upwards, can contribute to the vitality of all their faculties. In order to evolve, humans must learn to direct their energies towards the world of the soul and spirit: in this way, they will awaken faculties in their brain they are not yet aware of.

The genitals themselves are neutral, exactly like a fountain and a tap are neutral – what matters is the quality of the water that passes through them. What humans give through these organs depends on the nature of their thoughts, their feelings, and their level of consciousness. In those who have learned to sublimate sexual energy thanks to their constant aspiration to a higher life, this quintessence comes alive with intense vibrations – it is powerful and attracts heavenly beings that, through them, create a new life of light and beauty.

8 March

***P**eople who climb very high peaks find that up there, certain thoughts and certain selfish and petty feelings leave them. They find that many things that worried or hurt them seem suddenly irrelevant, thanks to the altitude, the pure air, and the space that opens wide in front of them.

The same is true with those who have grown spiritually. Up until then, like every human being, they were inhabited by lower entities that their dark thoughts and feelings had attracted. But the atmosphere that reigns in the regions of their spirit to where they have now risen is unbreathable for such entities – they cannot stand them, and so they leave. The higher we go, the freer we become, because with every step we make towards the summit, the entities that cannot survive beyond a certain altitude are forced to leave.

9 March

Humans believe that they will find peace by changing or removing something or someone exterior to them or that bothered them. And that's where they are wrong. Because peace is a state that we must first create within ourselves.

Do not imagine you will finally find peace by changing husband or wife, by moving apartment, changing friends, job, country, or religion, and so on. Peace does not depend on these kinds of changes. Some tranquility or a break, yes maybe. But in no time, other torments will come and assail you. You must understand that peace depends only on your ability to bring order to your psychic life. Make these changes and you will be able to stay with the same people in the same places, faced with the same challenges – nothing will perturb you anymore. For true peace comes from within: it pours fourth and overwhelms you despite the turbulence and commotion of the outside world. It is like a river of light that descends from higher ground and permeates your entire being.

10 March

*I*ncense has long been reserved to churches, but these days in the West, burning incense at home has almost become fashionable: people like to breathe the perfumed scents imagining that even if they are busy with prosaic activities, the air around them is sanctified. But it is best to know the symbolic meaning of incense and keep it for spiritual practices.

Incense gives off a scent when it burns. The burning is symbolic of sacrifice. All sacrifice is combustion: matter given to fire so that its fragrant emanations rise up to the Divine. For us, the act of burning really only has meaning if we transpose it on another plane, that is to say, if the matter we sacrifice is our own matter – our psychic matter. Those who endeavour to overcome their weaknesses purify their psychic matter with the spiritual fire of divine wisdom and love. Once purified, this matter emanates the most subtle fragrances.

11 March

*T*rue clairvoyance gives access to the realities of the spiritual world, that is to say, it enables people to pick up the most subtle elements in nature and in human souls. Clairvoyance, which consists in seeing past events or those to come, or seeing entities in the astral world, is not so extraordinary. Almost everyone can acquire it through certain exercises or by taking certain drugs; but these means do not take them very far and they even present great dangers to people's psyche.

Don't be mistaken, humans who see into the invisible can only pick up realities corresponding to the level of consciousness they themselves have attained. It is therefore not surprising that most clairvoyants see mainly future accidents, diseases and catastrophes, as well as the lower entities circulating among humans. You must go very high within you to be able to see spirits of light and heavenly beings. The only clairvoyance you must seek to achieve is the one that makes you like a crystal prism, a pure crystal that lets through the light.

12 March

*I*t is always difficult to decide what is good and what is not. Because something bad or wrong is not 'evil', and something good or right is not 'the good'. There are often events that at first seem catastrophic but turn out to be positive. And unfortunately, the opposite is also true: apparently happy events are transformed into catastrophes because people have neither the wisdom nor the mastery necessary to take advantage of these favourable situations.

When events occur, we cannot know whether with time, they will turn out to be beneficial or harmful to ourselves and to others. So when you suffer a setback or hardship, make the habit of telling yourself that down the line, something good might be waiting for you.

13 March

Christians are perhaps proud to belong to a religion that tells them that two thousand years ago God wanted to manifest his love by sending his only son to save them. Unfortunately, the belief that Jesus is the only son of God saves no one, and we must now dismiss this outrageous idea. For it also shows very poor understanding of God's love which is immense, eternal and infinite: God has had many sons and daughters, he has many at present, and there will be many more.

God has always accompanied humans with his love by sending them beings that help them evolve, and he will continue to send more. He has no interest in authorities that forbid him to send anyone else after Jesus or say that humans were derived of true light before Jesus came. As if the salvation of human beings depended on the era they lived in: before Jesus or after Jesus! The Church may persist in setting a beginning and an end to divine revelation, but the Lord is not deterred by such decrees, he continues to ignore them and to send his sons and daughters to save humanity.

14 March

When we see what most people call freedom, the word 'licence' or 'debauchery' would really be more suitable. So many people want to be free to give in to laziness, pleasure and passion, without realizing it is precisely this attitude that limits them and enslaves them! True freedom is not acquired by freeing oneself from all constraints, but by becoming a servant, yes, a servant of God.

Human beings' destiny is to find the Divine that dwells within them and to serve it. When their physical, psychic and spiritual faculties are fully imbued with the Divine they will become truly free – free and creative. There is something essential you must understand here. Those who serve the divine Principle do not serve someone or something exterior to themselves. That is why, not only do they not lose their freedom; on the contrary, they gain freedom. This is one of the main principles of true religion.

15 March

How often do you suffer when you learn that you have been criticized or accused unfairly? Your first reaction is obviously to respond, which is often useless, because we cannot stop people from talking and saying what suits them with no regard for the truth.

To avoid enduring gossip and slander, here is what you must do. Through thought and prayer, rise up to the regions in you where light reigns. There, the currents given off by this negative talk will no longer reach you: the law of backlash will take effect, and such talk will return to those who uttered the slander and they will be the ones to suffer its negative effects. This is how divine Justice manifests.

16 March

*E*ach time a human being makes a mistake, some entities present with them and in them, in their blood cells, in the cells of their muscles and organs, or in their nervous system, leave them. Up until then these entities served them, but now they refuse to do so, and they can even turn against them. Each transgression brings disorder to certain cells in their body: because they are related to this person and depend on them, they are continually influenced by this person's behaviour. And because this person is so rarely aware of the consequences of their actions, they continue to create conflict first and foremost in their body. And so one day, their stomach no longer obeys them, neither do their lungs, their liver, their legs, nor their head, nothing. And even enemies can sneak inside them and torment them. They are being told, 'You're not on the right path, you must act differently.'

Through their disorderly life, humans make enemies who take every opportunity to harm them. But if they begin to settle down, to respect the laws of nature, and to lead a sensible and harmonious life, their enemies will become their friends again.

17 March

*T*here are people who say they have faith and practise a religion. That's all well and good, but why are they still so weak and wobbly? Because they believe that they must seek God somewhere, far away, in what they call heaven. They don't know that in reality God is in them, not only in their soul and spirit, but in every particle in their body.

It is very important you become aware of God's presence in you. The mere thought of his presence in you brings order, balance and harmony to your entire being. Even if you are not yet very strong, even if you sometimes feel confused and make mistakes, as long as you remain aware of God's presence, you will progress under the guidance of a reliable guide.

18 March

Parents must be aware of their responsibilities. They do not have the right to invite a soul to incarnate in their family if they are unable to live up to their task. Bringing children into the world is not only a personal and private affair, because each time, the future of humanity depends on this act.

This is why it is not the education of children that worries me most, but that of parents. I would like to make them understand that bringing children into the world should not be limited to expressing an atavistic instinct of procreation. This instinct of course exists in everyone and it cannot be rooted out, but it must be understood in a more conscious and more spiritual light. Unlike animals that only reproduce, humans have the possibility of realizing a true act of creation, but only on condition they engage their thought, their soul and their spirit. Any creation depends on the creators themselves, and they can, and must improve themselves, so that their creations surpass them.

19 March

*T*he diamond has a lustre that puts it above all other precious stones. Our spirit, like a diamond, is pure light, and it is toward this light shining at the summit of our being that we must rise by working to acquire true simplicity.

Simplicity is primarily a quality of our intellect, and this requires us to vibrate in unison with the divine Principle. From there, it descends into our heart to purify our feelings and desires. And finally, our will, putting itself in service of our intellect and heart, brings order and harmony everywhere. It is obviously difficult to achieve this simplicity. Much knowledge and great effort is required to rid ourselves of all the foreign and contradictory elements that are mixed and entangled in human beings. If a spiritual teaching gives us so many explanations, methods, and exercises, it is to show us how to acquire true simplicity so that we may become diamonds.

20 March

During the course of a year, the sun passes through four cardinal points: the vernal equinox on 21 March; the summer solstice on 21 June; the autumn equinox on 21 September; the winter solstice on 21 December. These are four moments in nature when there are large influxes of energies affecting all forms of life.

On the wheel of the Zodiac, spring begins with Aries, a fire sign; summer begins with Cancer, a water sign; autumn with Libra, an air sign; and winter with an earth sign, Capricorn. Therefore, the start of each season is linked with one of the four elements. Each element is governed by powerful entities who command myriad of servants responsible for spreading the new currents of energy accross the surface of the planet. The universe is not a machine, and the movements that drive it are not set off mechanically: each change is produced by the work of living beings invisible to us, with the responsibility of taking particular care of stones, plants, animals, or humans.

21 March

*E*ach year, when spring returns and the warmth and light increase, all the seeds in the ground begin to sprout and grow. It is a time for us to think about all the seeds within us: they are also ready to germinate and grow under the light and warmth of the sun – the spiritual sun. The sun we see rising on the horizon each morning is a distant reflection of this spiritual sun. By learning to focus on the sun, we connect ourselves to the spiritual sun that vivifies the seeds the Creator planted in us.

Each morning, by consciously presenting ourselves before the sun, we become the gardeners of our own earth. The small shoots – the qualities and virtues of our heavenly Father – need to be watered. The sun sends its light and warmth, but cannot water the plants. It is our role to water them with the water within us: our love and gratitude. Every progress we make in this endeavour is inscribed within us, and we will feel its benefit throughout our life, and even beyond, in our future lives.

22 *March*

*G*od waits for all creatures to return to him – even those known as the rebel angels are not cast out forever. God told them, 'You chose to distance yourselves from me? All right, you were free. But the day you have suffered enough from living in darkness and limitation, come back, and I will welcome you.' Such is God's love. He never refuses to welcome the guilty who wish to return to him.

Do not believe the rebel angels are happy to live far from God; they suffer. It is pride that prevents them from recognizing their errors, but the door remains open to them. When they repent and cease to harm humans, they will regain their place, and their leader, Lucifer, will once again be the archangel of light.

23 March

So many ascetics and mystics have taken on a life of deprivation on the pretext that the physical body is the tomb of the spirit. No, it is simply up to humans not to let their body bury their spirit. To do so, they must put their body in service of their spirit, because their body and their spirit have work to do together.

The spirit and the body are like heaven and earth, and in the 'Our Father' prayer, Jesus emphasized the relationship that must exist between them,

'Our Father, who art in heaven,
hallowed be thy name (hallowed by humans).
Thy kingdom come (settle among them),
thy will be done on earth as it is in heaven."

Carrying out God's will is to establish a link between earth and heaven so that the order, harmony, and light that prevail on high may descend and manifest down below, that is to say, in us too. Because if every human being does not make the effort to instil these qualities in themselves first, it is useless to hope to see them manifest in the world.

24 March

*T*here is one word uniting the Creator to Creation, a word that also unites all creatures – the word 'life'. Life is the very quintessence that God, in the beginning, drew from himself to create the universe and all the beings that inhabit it.

Beings and the created universe exist thanks to the life of God. When some people claim they require proof the Creator exists in order for them to believe in him, one wonders about the degree of blindness and obscurity of their consciousness. Where do they think this life they see and feel in them and around them comes from? If they meditate on life and its countless manifestations, they will no longer need proof that God exists. Since life is also a mystery that no one is truly able to explain, as they make their way through this mystery that is life, they will also progress in the mystery of the Lord.

25 March

So many disciples wait for their Master to reveal what they must do to become clairvoyants, alchemists, cabbalists, mages, and so on. They don't realize that this kind of desire has no real utility and can even be of harm to them. Aquiring occult knowledge and powers is what should come last. And wanting to start with what comes last is a very bad trend among disciples of an initiatic teaching. They don't know anything about the psychic and spiritual worlds and have not purified themselves, but they are greedy to receive the biggest secrets of initiation. These great secrets will crush them, they will not be able to endure them; but they don't see that and they don't want to see that.

Simply being interested in occult science does not suffice. All true Masters will tell you that. But the day a Master sees that someone is ready, they themselves will bring down the veil and make everything the disciple wished to know accessible to them.

26 March

Humans have the habit of responding to evil with evil and to hatred with hatred, but this old philosophy has never produced good results. So often, in trying to get rid of an enemy, they actually tie themselves to their enemy! Because when we hate someone, it's exactly as if we love them. People think that hatred cuts ties. On the contrary, it creates ties as strong and as firm as love. These ties are of course different: love brings certain things, and hatred brings others but just as surely and as powerfully as love does.

All that is good opposes evil, and it is thanks to love that we can fight hatred. Evil is always defeated in the end, for God refused to make it immortal. We can compare every word and act of hatred to a stone thrown up in the air – with time, it has less force to rise up. Conversely, a good word or an act of kindness can be compared to a stone thrown from the top of a tower – with time, its movement and power gain impetus. This is the secret of all that is good: although it may be weak at first, in the end it is all-powerful and triumphant.

27 *March*

Blood is always associated with the idea of life, and it is even one of the most powerful symbols of life. While it circulates in the body blood is protected as if in a sealed container. But as soon as it flows out of the body for whatever reason, like any liquid, it evaporates, that is to say the etheric particles it emanates are dispersed in the atmosphere. And because these particles retain some of the elements that make blood lifegiving, they are food for invisible entities.

Nothing is lost in the universe: there are always good or evil entities that come to feed off the life emanating from even a few drops of blood. So, when you lose blood, do not let it dry and do not get rid of it until you have dedicated it in thought to that which is good. In dedicating it in this way, you repel the dark entities on the astral plane always seeking to feed on blood's emanations to strengthen themselves, and you attract beings of light.

28 March

***H**ow can humans be taught to control their thoughts and desires so that they stop polluting the etheric nature and regions? They are not vigilant enough to avoid polluting the physical plane right before their eyes, and are even less so with regards to the psychic plane which they do not see; they continue emitting bad thoughts and feelings that permeate the people they spend time with. And maybe these people's consciousness is not sufficiently elevated for them to sense the noxious elements that enter them either; even if they are not aware of these elements, they take immediate effect. And since everything is recorded, those who sent them will one day be punished.

We must always seek to live in harmony with this great universal body that gives us 'free room and boarding' and strive to fill space with pure, luminous, and good thoughts. Since these purifying currents do not remain in one place only, they will be a blessing for the whole of humanity.

29 March

When you plant a seed in the ground, for it to grow, it must first divide: it becomes 2. Then the sprout contained within it draws the elements it needs from both the halves that feed it: it becomes 3. Soon after that, only the seed coat is left and it too will eventually disappear. Here we witness the seed's death, and this death is necessary for new life to be born. In dying, the seed releases the powers of life it contains.

In human beings, it is their lower self that must die so as to feed the divine principle that can then grow, blossom and bear fruit. Nature never ceases to teach us about life, that is to say about death and resurrection. For what we call life, is really only an uninterrupted series of death and resurrection. Death is always the promise of new life, and this life itself will be followed by death so that new life can once again be born. This is really what resurrection is.

30 March

*Y*ou have loved someone: from the very first moments you experienced wonder, poetry and music. The mere thought that the other person existed and that you might see them in the street or elsewhere was enough for you. You were once able to acquire an object they had touched or that had belonged to them, and even if it was something insignificant, for you it was the most precious treasure in the world because it was infused with their emanations: it was like a talisman. Then, you started to see each other and things took their 'usual' course, as they say. At the time, you no doubt tasted other pleasures and joys, but you lost that magical something you had experienced in your first encounters. And it all often ended in disappointment, misunderstanding and separation.

You must understand that maintaining love does not reside in physically possessing someone; it resides in something subtle that, through the other person, links us to the universe and to the beauty of earth and heaven.

31 March

*I*n the morning we go to contemplate the sun rising. In doing so, we eat it and drink it, and its living light and warmth spread to all the cells in our body enlightening them, strengthening them, purifying them and vivifying them.

Every day, you are before the sun which projects particles of light into space. By looking at it, imagine that you free yourselves of your body's impurities to replace them with the particles of light the sun sends you. With all your heart, with all your soul, take these divine particles and place them within you. And so, little by little, thanks to the sun, you will impregnate the matter of your being with spiritual vibrations and become more and more alive.

1 April

***D**isciples of an initiatic teaching have a clear understanding of the laws of destiny. They know that the hardships they will encounter in their lifetime are the result of their wrongdoings in past incarnations, and that they must make amends and learn. To do so, they must accept all the conditions divine Justice has decreed for them, for nothing can oppose such decrees. If they suffer a setback, fall sick or make a bad encounter, they cannot escape these situations because they are not free on the physical plane.

But human beings do not only live on the physical plane – freedom is also, and above all, acquired on the spiritual plane. If through prayer and meditation, you connect with the divine world, if you work to increase your light, strength, purity and love, when you are faced with difficult times, you will be able to transform them: you will consider and bear the hardships differently without feeling overwhelmed, and you will instead feel encouraged and enriched by them.

2 April

*I*t is really difficult for human beings to truly know themselves – they represent such an immense and diverse world. Having been made in God's image, humans are found throughout Creation. And because they are unaware of this, their life is very difficult. Particularly when they clash with others and bump things without knowing that these other people are part of them and that they are part of others. This truth is the basis of moral code.

All laws about respect and love of one's neighbour are based on the fact that what people do to others, they also do to themselves. Even if they are not aware of this due to their limited and obscured consciousness, the suffering they inflict on their fellow humans also affects them; by destroying something in others, they unknowingly destroy something in themselves. So often they feel faint or experience various disorders without knowing the reason why. These are simply the repercussions of the harm they thought they had only done to others.

3 April

Some people seek a spiritual Master because they believe that by living close to someone who has achieved great elevation, they will be favoured: not only they will be protected when they are with him, but merely through his presence they will receive his knowledge and powers. But this is not true. A spiritual Master teaches truths and gives methods, but it is up to the disciples to apply them, and to work for their own freedom and salvation. They will only progress through the efforts they themselves make.

The Creator desires one thing only: for human beings to improve themselves. And they must work in order to better themselves. A spiritual Master sets an example for his disciples, he opens up the path for them and tells them how to walk, but he cannot walk for them – the disciples must walk for themselves. Even if a Master is able to do so, he will not carry a disciple on his shoulders, for this will teach them nothing and they will remain weak. And if he does happen to intervene in a disciple's life, it is to provide particular help and because he knows that his disciple will then be able to walk alone.

4 April

Colours are modulations of light and through them, entities working in stones, plants, animals, and humans manifest themselves. By concentrating on colours, you can bring them alive in you: they help you develop virtues related to them and they support you in your endeavours.

Remember to use the means nature offers you to connect with the spiritual world. Colours are one of these means. Take the colour blue for example – it is the color of peace and truth. From time to time, immerse yourself in this colour. Imagine that you are surrounded by blue rays and feel them permeate you: little by little, you will feel a deep sense of peace overcome you. This deep peace will at last silence your heart and intellect and will help you to free yourselves of your greed, prejudice and bias, and everything will become clearer to you. Heaven is reflected in your soul as if on the still surface of a lake, and with this deep sense of peace, you will contemplate the truth.

5 April

*L*ife is transmitted and perpetuated by the sexual organs. You must study the science and wisdom that goes into creating these organs, and respect them. However, they are often the organs which are the least respected: puritans consider them with disgust, the debauched abuse them, comedians and rude people joke about them, and most men and women see them simply as a source of enjoyment.

Initiatic Science tells us that the energy that manifests through the genitals descends from the heavenly regions. And because this energy descends from the heavenly regions, humans would do well to think about how they use their organs that enable this energy to manifest. They should even dedicate them to the Divine, so that, instead of allowing this energy to simply pass through them and go to waste, this cosmic energy of love may rise up and vivify all the cells in their body, including their brain. If they are content with feeling this energy like a great tension which they are eager to release, they deprive themselves of all the joy love could bring them, and of all the knowledge and power too.

6 April

There are two methods you can use to progress: love and wisdom. If you meet people who possess these virtues that you yourself have not yet been able to develop sufficiently, instead of avoiding them because you feel they offend you, draw near to them and observe their behaviour: you will learn a lot this way. There are people who cannot stand the moral and spiritual superiority of certain people, and they have mixed negative feelings about them: irritation, envy, revolt, and so on. But such feelings do not help them, for they only maintain their stagnation.

Only love and wisdom can help us progress quickly. Some people fear that others may outshine them or they are jealous of those who have surpassed them – this simply reveals that they have neither love nor wisdom. With love and wisdom, we are never worried or jealous: because we feel rich. Why would rich people want to be envious? Only the poor can be envious because they feel helpless. But obviously I'm referring to spiritual wealth and poverty.

7 April

*G*iving life is an enormous responsibility. Therefore, before conceiving a child, men and women must reflect and above all prepare themselves, knowing well that bringing a child into the world does not only mean they add another person to the world's population. Parents, through their inner states, attract either the soul of someone who will be very beneficial to humanity, or of someone mediocre who will be of no help to others, or worse still, of a criminal.

'And what if we don't have children, if we don't become a father or mother?' you might ask. Know that there are other ways of bringing children into the world, on other planes. When you go to attend the sunrise in the morning, instill within you the importance of what you go to do there, and for what purpose. The sun is like a father who deposits seeds in hearts and souls, and everyone therefore becomes a mother. If you welcome these seeds with respect and love, the children you bear will be called clarity, strength, and inspiration. These are the children the cosmic Father, the sun, can create in hearts and souls.

8 April

Human beings' lower nature is like an enemy who continues to destroy the good work they have done. Despite them seeking to transform their being into a land where vegetation will grow to nourish themselves as well as others, their lower nature strives to sow the seeds of poisonous plants in them: jealousy, pride, sensuality, greed, vanity, anger, and so on. And why does it so often succeed? Because humans are neither educated nor vigilant.

Try to identify this inner enemy seeking to sneak through and sow weeds or even poisonous plants in you. By studying the methods it uses you will be warned of its arrival. Because there are warning signs whenever it comes near: a thought, an image, a feeling, a desire. If you fall prey to it, it is because you have not analysed yourself well; you are just walking about on the surface of your own being, waiting for great hardships so you can start worrying about what is happening within you. Now that you have been warned, you will be better able to observe yourself so as to notice the clues announcing your enemy's imminent arrival.

9 April

Humans have always felt the need to seek their reasons for living in the outside, physical and material world. Thanks to the possibilities now offered by science and technology, our contemporaries throw themselves headlong into exploiting all the resources nature provides them. If they were to accept to further develop their inner capacities, not only would they have less need to plunder the planet's resources to the detriment of earth's populations, they would also understand that their inner riches are inexhaustible and infinite, unlike the planet's material riches.

The Creator placed in all those he created, the subtle equivalent of everything that can be found in the universe. So instead of monopolozing and exhausting the earth, why don't humans turn more to the wealth they already possess – the wealth of spirit? Everything they then achieve on the physical plane will be marked with the seal of spirit, and they will know how to treat nature with care and intelligence.

10 April

A criminal preparing their crime knows they must hide their intentions and work in the dark. So how can people with good intentions expect to succeed if they expose themselves in plain daylight? How naive they are. Some people are vain and show off, and in so doing they provoke opposition and arouse spite and jealousy. Whether you intend to do something good or bad, it is best not to attract attention – that's how things work.

If you are thinking of giving someone a gift, be careful, for it would be best if there were no witnesses. And sometimes, it might even be preferable if the person you are benefitting does not know where the gift comes from, for your gesture might provoke unexpected reactions in them that they will not know how to interpret. Wanting to do good does not suffice: for then too, it is sometimes necessary to take precautions.

11 April

*L*ife is the strongest bond there is between a father and his children. Not only do all fathers hope their children will not waste the life he has given them, they also hope they will put it to good use and live a good and meaningful life. The same is true of God: he gave us life and he asks nothing more of us than to respect this treasure given to us for a period of time. For it is his life, and he expects us to make it bear fruit by giving it new colours, new scents and flavours.

This God-given life manifests in us through qualities, gifts and virtues, and we will one day be asked to account for the way we have used them. If we neglect to use them, we will lose them. For we lose anything we don't put to good use. But if we develop our gifts for the benefit of others, we will be rewarded and will receive even more precious ones.

12 April

If we compare humans to animals, it's surprising how quickly a little animal grows and becomes independant, while human children grow so slowly. This slowness is due to human nature's extreme wealth and complexity. Physically and psychically especially, so many mechanisms must develop for children to acquire all the necessary abilities. And until they do, they require the help and protection of their parents.

But human evolution does not stop when their earthly father and mother have fulfilled their role. Human beings are also spiritual beings that must continually progress. This is why, even once they have reached adulthood, they are still like a child who needs their parents spiritually speaking: their heavenly Father and divine Mother. Regardless of their knowledge and experience, every human must stay young at heart, like a child – simple, spontaneous, open, and totally trusting of their heavenly parents so as to receive their help and advice.

13 April

When people talk about the devil, they do not know exactly to what cosmic or psychic reality this word corresponds. Firstly, the devil does not exist as an entity opposed to God and on an equal footing with him. Those who claim the devil appeared to them have only imagined it. Spirits of light exist and so do spirits of darkness. It is this group of dark spirits that we call the devil, and this collective force is nourished and reinforced by people's negative thoughts, feelings and actions.

We can also say that the devil is a part of human beings themselves: their lower self that they have continuously fed during their reincarnations by reason of their weaknesses and vices. However, an entity of light also exists in humans: their higher self formed thanks to their thoughts, feelings and actions inspired by kindness, generosity, love and sacrifice. Throughout their lives, humans are torn between their lower self and their higher self, and it's up to them to decide which of the two they would like to see materialize.

14 April

Seeing communion as something to be celebrated only in a church or a temple restricts its meaning. A greater and broader meaning should be given to communion. For it is the condition for life itself. To commune is also to eat, drink, breathe, walk, watch, listen, love, work and to seek constantly to interact with living creatures and forces of nature.

Every act of daily life can become a way of experiencing magnificent states of consciousness that are ways of communing. It is even all these forms of communion which give meaning to Christian communion. The day we understand what true communion is, in its cosmic dimension, we will feel currents of abundant and pure energy circulating in all regions of our being, and we will know what eternal life without beginning or end is.

15 April

***H**umans don't really need a religion or a spiritual teaching to impose laws on them. Above all, they need methods to help them discover the living imprint God has left in them. Fortunately, they all bear this imprint. And when they truly seek it, it enables them to find, in their heart and soul, what religions don't always reveal to them. Why? Because far too many of those who represent religions are more concerned with maintaining their power than with enlightening the faithful, even though they say they lead them on the path to salvation.

How can we understand what God's imprint is? When he created us, he marked us with his seal, imbued us with his quintessence, and left fluidic traces in us, together with a whole network of filaments connecting us to him, thanks to which, if we make the effort to search for him, we will find him.

16 April

*T*he atmosphere surrounding earth and divided by science into various layers, each with a particular name (troposphere, stratosphere, and so on), extends for several hundred kilometres into space. But beyond that, earth has an etheric body which extends right out to the sun – it touches the sun and merges with its etheric body. For the sun too possesses an etheric body which, extending well beyond its own sphere, touches earth, and further still, the other planets. This is why the sun and earth are not separate, their atmospheres connect and melt into each other.

And since human beings are formed in the image of the universe, they too touch the sun on the subtle plane of emanations. Even if you cannot yet sense it, tell yourself that there is a part of you, a very subtle part – your higher self – that dwells in the sun.

17 April

Like all exceptional beings, initiates are inevitably misunderstood, opposed, and even betrayed. But to overcome such tests, they know they must not defend themselves with ordinary weapons. They only strive to live a pure, luminous and radiant life, and this life not only acts as a protective layer, but also causes evil to return to those who sent it. They need do nothing more than rise up toward the heavenly regions to live even more in the light.

Here is what you must do when you are wrongy attacked. Distance yourselves as much as possible from your adversaries. When heaven sees that you are not behaving like them, it may send other people to take action instead of you and restore the situation. As for you, simply continue to broaden, embellish, enrich and illuminate your life.

18 April

***R**eligions that have not encouraged a sense of martyrdom among their followers are rare. Followers should now be encouraged to cease acts such as manhandling and mutilating their body and endangering their life in sacrifice to the Divine.

True sacrifice is found in selfless love for all humans. Those who have understood the meaning and power of love don't need to inflict suffering upon themselves: there is already enough to be shared with their misfortunate brothers and sisters. And the obstacles they will encounter in their efforts to help others present them with yet more opportunities to suffer. But they must not retreat when faced with this suffering: for it will make them grow and ennoble them.

19 April

*A*lchemy is the science of the transformation of matter. In the crucible, the alchemist places the prima materia, the base matter, which, initially, dies and rots down; this operation corresponds to the colour black. Next, the matter is dissolved and purified and becomes white. Then come distillation and conjunction where the matter turns red, and finally, sublimation where the colour turns to gold. These operations are only meaningful to us if we see them as different stages of our inner life.

The work alchemists perform on the matter in a crucible is, in fact, the work of regeneration disciples perform in the crucible of their own body, a work to which they must devote their entire life. The regenerated matter comes out of the crucible transformed into gold: a regenerated human has died to their lower nature to been born to their higher nature. This is also the meaning when Jesus said, *'Unless a grain of wheat falls into the earth and dies, it remains just a single grain; but if it dies, it bears much fruit.'* This sentence can be taken as a summary of the alchemical process: dying to our lower nature so as to bear the fruit of our higher nature.

20 April

*W*e don't have to wait for the end of time to leave our tomb and rise again. To resurrect, we must simply work on ourselves every day in order to overcome all our weaknesses. This work has an effect on the cells in our body – it purifies them, enlightens them and vivifies them. Increasingly intense vibrations are gradually communicated to all our cells and prepare our resurrection.

If only humans knew the number of tombs they have within them. These tombs are all the cells they must regenerate by learning how to nourish themselves with elements of spiritual life. And so, one by one, the tombs open and numerous little souls who were seemingly dead, but who in reality were dormant, begin to rise up. Similar phenomena are present everywhere in nature. A seed is a tomb in which life remains buried until the angel of spring knocks on the door to release it. The same is true of the eggshell and the chick. The custom of offering Easter eggs of course exists because the egg symbolizes the promise of a new life.

21 April

*A*ll of nature resurrects in spring. But resurrection is also a continuous process taking place in the souls of those who work on themselves with awareness and enlightenment towards a divine goal. And such a process necessarily begins with our head. This means that if we place a very elevated idea at the centre of our life, and if we firmly maintain it within us, this idea will attract, from the subtle planes, etheric particles in harmony with it: rustproof like gold and transparent like crystal.

Most importantly, begin with an idea. But it can also be an image that embodies this idea, like the image of the sun. If you hold within you the image of the sun – which is light, warmth and life – you are already on the path to resurrection. Maintain it steadfastly, nourish it and love it, and it will do its job. Resurrection is the sun that begins to manifest itself in humans – the true sun bringing them a quintessence of its own nature, like leaven and ferment.

22 April

From the moment we fall asleep our soul moves away from our physical body and goes to join the universal Soul. During the body's rest, an entire process of cleansing and purification takes place. Subtle ties known as the 'silver cord' keep the soul connected to the physical body when it leaves it. On its return, the soul finds the house swept, cleaned and washed, and it can take up its work again.

If the soul did not leave the body in this way, we would die from poisoning and asphyxiation, because the work of cleansing could not be done. You may wonder where these toxins and poisons come from. They are produced quite simply because life is a combustion. All the physical, emotional and mental activities we know as 'life' give off forces, but they also leave behind impurities which take a while to be eliminated. So it is necessary for the soul to withdraw from the body so the cleansing can take place. Sleep is the solution that cosmic Intelligence has found so that we can continue to live.

23 *April*

Humans can be compared to fruit trees: their circumstances are like the ground on which they must grow, blossom and bear fruit. How many people, after suffering great hardship and believing they would not survive, have had to admit that such events made them, let's say, more 'productive'. This is because they were forced not only to seek resources within themselves, but also to learn how to use them.

Rather than complaining about difficult conditions, wanting to change them or expecting better ones at any cost, start by working on yourselves: dig deep into yourselves to find the elements, powers and virtues that will make you bear the most succulent fruit.

24 April

Unlike the generally accepted theory, humans did not descend from the ape or any other animal. Billions of years ago when earth's crust solidified, plants appeared, followed by animals, and finally by humans. Evolution certainly took place from plants to humans, but it was only their forms that evolved. The human spirit descended only when a form that suited it emerged. This can be likened to a new house owner who takes possession of a house only once it has finished being built for them. It's not the house that produces the owner, they are not created by the walls of the house! They arrive from somewhere else and do not move in until the house is ready.

In the same way, when the spirit found a body capable of receiving it and also the right conditions to manifest through this body, it descended from the heavenly regions and, as it has done for millions of years now, it keeps descending. The evolution of forms was necessary for the involution of spirit to take place.

25 April

T*ry taking two pieces of wood and rubbing them together. Very quickly this friction generates heat, and if you continue you will soon see small flames appear – this is light. Movement, heat and light are three steps that have their equivalent in our psychic life: movement (will, action) produces heat (feeling, love), and heat produces light (thought, understanding).

The conclusion to be made is that you must not neglect the exercises given by a spiritual teaching. When you receive knowledge, love it enough to put it into practice. Little by little, you will feel warmth awaken in you, and you will acquire a taste for this knowledge to the point you will soon be unable to go without it. When this heat turns into light, you will receive enlightenment to help you better guide your life.

26 April

*H*aving observed some negative effects of the influence of families on their children, some thinkers have claimed to remedy this by calling the family's presence into question: in their opinion, it was no longer the family's role to ensure the child's education, but that of state controlled institutions. Well, these are misconceptions that can only create serious problems for children as well as for parents. For their development, children need to feel the presence of their parents, and parents need to take care of their children. A state or an institution will never solve children's education problems by removing them from their parents and placing them in the care of strangers. Of course, I am not talking about exceptional circumstances where parents are unable to care for their children.

Not only should children be allowed to live with their parents, but parents must be very present for their children and be aware of their responsibilities in the upbringing they give them. And the first of these responsibilities is to set good examples for them.

27 April

*P*recious stones are the culmination of all transformation work done by the intelligence of nature on the raw material the earth carries within it; as if they wanted to not only reflect, but also to materialize the light and the splendour of heaven. This is why in many religions and spiritualist movements, precious stones are considered as symbols of divine virtues. They represent this ideal towards which we must strive in endeavouring to transmute the raw material – our instincts.

Precious stones represent en entire teaching because they are connected to the spiritual world. Learn to focus on them, on their purity, on their colours and their power to let the light pass through them, ask them to enter within you with all their properties and virtues, nourish yourselves with their quintessences and may the brilliant sparkle of sapphires, diamonds, rubies, emeralds, and the topaz illuminate your entire being.

28 April

*Y*ou may sometimes wonder whether it is so important to set yourselves a discipline in life in order to reach a higher level of consciousness, and to develop mastery, wisdom and kindness. For it takes much time and effort. Of course you can live on earth without imposing so much effort on yourselves. It's evident every day – we can live on earth just about anyhow. But the question is: what 'earth' do we live on then? In order to live in the land of our soul, this region where it is forever spring, we must feed our spiritual bodies.

On the earth where we presently live it is impossible to escape winter, with its cold, its clouds and rain. But through thought we can already rise up to the region of this eternal spring. And when we are able reach our higher self, nothing can ever come between us and the divine sun – we will always be enlightened, warmed and vivified.

29 April

*T*o survive, all creatures need to feed themselves, but once they have done so, they must eliminate the elements that are no longer useful to their bodies. So, whatever the quality of what they take in, there is waste to be evacuated and it is shipped to places specially provided for this. These processes are found on all planes and at all levels of Creation. Thus, hell, which Christians have spoken so much about for centuries, depicting it in frightening forms and colours, is actually the place where all that is 'evil' – that is to say the waste and the impure matter produced and released by all creatures in the universe – is dumped.

But once there, this matter is not abandoned and forgotten. Powerful entities descend into this depository to collect items they will reuse for their work. Nature has always carried out what we today call 'recycling': since nothing must remain unused, nature sends all polluted matter to the treatment plant.

30 April

*I*n exercising their job, many doctors think that calling on the knowledge they learnt from books is sufficient: they lean over their patient just like mechanics who service a car – and their care will certainly have a beneficial effect. But take a doctor with great kindness and compassion: their behaviour is infused with these qualities. So when they are with their patients, everything emanating from their eyes, their voice, and their handshake, awakens forces in their patient's heart and soul that will imperceptibly act on their psychic bodies and even have as beneficial an effect on their physical body as would medicine.

In all areas of life, we see that what emanates from very deep down in people has an effect on the psychic matter of those close to them, and on all those these people in turn come into contact with. You yourselves have noticed this. Are there not people that you particularly appreciate being with, because simply through their presence you feel better yourselves, you become smarter and more confident in life, and you even feel better physically?

1 May

Creation, with its myriad manifestations and events, can in fact be reduced to a set of numbers. If we succeed in vivifying numbers, understanding how they work, we can see they represent forces that act in nature, and their sums, subtractions, multiplications and divisions produce forms and movement. When we look at a snail's shell or the structure of a crystal, how can we not admire the work of numbers? All the principles of arithmetic are found in stones, plants, animals, stars, in the human body, in humans' psychic life, and even in their destiny.

Numbers are therefore at the origin of creation: each existence is the result of the crystallisation and aggregation of material elements around a number. Those who succeed in acquiring the true science of numbers are not only capable of piercing the mysteries of creation, they also possess the omnipotence of the spirit, for numbers are the primary expression of the spirit.

2 *May*

Solomon said *'There is nothing new under the sun'*. Perhaps, but isn't the sun itself always new? Each morning, as it rises, it invites us to receive new life, to harmonise ourselves with the new currents that it sends throughout the universe. And why remain under the sun? If by thought we seek to ascend into the sun, if we enter into vibration with its heart, then everything will seem new to us each day.

At first, it is obviously difficult to perceive the sun as a living, vibrant being. You look at it and it seems far away to you. Why? Because it is not a part of you, or rather, because you have not yet been able to become a part of it. But persevere, strive to enter into it, soon you will receive new forces from it. It will be as if, for the first time, you are finally living.

3 May

We must never forget that reality manifests itself as two opposing aspects: there is the pure and the impure, darkness and light, good and evil. True knowledge encompasses both. That is why all real initiates must measure themselves against the powers of evil. It is not enough for them to know and work with good, they also explore evil, they 'descend into hell', those regions traditionally called the netherworld. They prepare themselves for a long time, and once properly armed, taking great precautions, they decide to face this netherworld and its inhabitants.

Some bold spirits have sought to venture into these regions, but they were not yet up to the task. This is where the formula 'to know, to will, to dare, to keep silent' that initiates have passed down among themselves through the centuries takes on its full meaning. Once initiates have acquired the necessary knowledge, they have the will to act. They then dare to confront the powers of evil. And when they have claimed victory, they keep silent, because it is dangerous to speak of hell to humans who are not ready to hear of it: some might be frightened and others might embark on very risky experiments.

4 May

***B**eyond being this red liquid that circulates in our body, blood is a subtle, life-bearing fluid, a condensation of precious essences. Even though, chemically, the blood of all humans is made up of identical elements, not all creatures have the same blood: its quality depends on their way of living, their qualities and virtues, and their degree of evolution. This should make you aware of the importance of the blood circulating inside your body, to meditate on the powers with which it is imbued.

Initiates can discover the quintessence of matter in a drop of blood, the principles of the four elements: earth, water, air and fire. Blood represents the life that circulates throughout the universe, and blood is that within us which most closely resembles light. It is therefore with the utmost respect that we must consider our own blood which is condensed light, condensed divine life. And just as blood returns to the heart, so too must our life return to the heart of the universe, the Creator.

5 May

*F*irstly, a temple is a building that isolates from profane space to create a holy place, a sanctuary for the Divine. It is good to build such places – temples, churches, synagogues or any other place of worship – so that humans, casting aside their daily prosaic preoccupations, can go there, conscious that their spirit and soul will receive nourishment. The atmosphere of reverence created by all those in attendance, as well as by all those who came before them to meditate, pray and sing in this temple, attracts heavenly beings, and each person then leaves regenerated, purified, enlightened, and at peace.

However, it is foremost within ourselves that we must build this sacred space in order to receive the Divine. The power of a prayer does not depend on the place where it is uttered. If your inner sanctuary has fallen into neglect, your prayers will not be heard. But if, through thoughts, feelings and acts inspired by wisdom and love, you have purified and illuminated your sanctuary, your voice will rise up to heaven wherever you may be.

6 May

*E*very morning, the rising sun marks the beginning of a day, and if you have plans, you are free to realize them or not, and to change them. But the moment the sun sets, when the day is over, what is done is done, nothing more, nothing less. Sunset represents the end of the cycle that is a day. However, in the language of symbols, a day is not only a twenty-four hour period; it can also represent a month, a year, and even a lifetime.

Every human being is given a sufficient amount of time to fulfil their obligations and make amends. Once this time has passed, anyone who has been negligent, who has shown ill-will or who, having done wrong, has not mended their mistakes, will suffer the law of karma. When we have not put our affairs in order before the sun sets, which is to say before leaving the earth, we will encounter the same difficulties in a future incarnation. And 'putting our affairs in order' means restoring harmonious relationships not only with the people around us, but with the divine world.

7 May

*T*hose who decide to go within discover that the source of their wealth – their spirit – is inexhaustible and that with very little, they are replete, fulfilled, and their thirst is quenched. It always comes back to the same question: how to free the spirit within us. It is first and foremost upon the spirit that we must rely. In times of trouble and hardship, only the spirit has the power to support us and give us the means to rebuild ourselves. Everyone can abandon us, we can lose everything, everything that is, except for ourselves, our spirit. So, why not search there, within, since it is the only possession, the only certainty we truly have?

Everything – our successes and joys, of course, but also our hardships and sorrows – can help us to seek the riches the spirit has placed within us. They may not be very apparent, for that which is most precious and given to us by the Creator is buried deep within us. But thanks to the effort we make to discover these riches, we will grow in the world of the spirit.

8 May

When you say that someone is lukewarm, it is usually not a compliment, it means you never know what to expect from them. Can you trust them? Should you be wary? In everyday life, dealing with such beings is complicated, because you cannot predict to which side they will lean.

Try this experiment: immerse your left hand in hot water for a moment and your right hand in cold water; each of your hands gradually reaches the temperature of the water in which it is immersed. Now place both hands in lukewarm water: you will see that your left hand finds it cold, while your right hand finds it hot. It is therefore impossible to tell: is the tepid water hot or cold? Similarly, if you are satisfied with 'lukewarm' thoughts and feelings, you can never have a clear idea about anything, and everything you do is indecisive, wavering.

9 May

*T*he psychic space surrounding the earth naturally rids it of the inferior entities that encumber it; they are warded off and absorbed into the underground depths. However, there still remain a few, and it is often they who manifest during spiritualist meetings.

It is within the ability of the lowest entities to enter into the head of a medium and speak in the name of Moses, Jesus, Joan of Arc or Napoleon; the name it uses to present itself proves nothing. Such entities manifesting themselves in this way come from the lower astral plane and often take malicious pleasure in deceiving humans. So, people who believe that they are enlightened by the answers they receive go further and further astray, and often end up suffering serious imbalances. It is not forbidden to attend spiritualist meetings to get an idea of what goes on there, but remain cautious, do not be too gullible.

10 May

*T*o give and take, or to receive and give back are like the two pans of a scale. When you take or receive, you must give something in return to restore balance. And even if you are not given anything, give! Why? Because that way you trigger a movement, and you receive something in return.

If you really want something good to remain of your time on earth, make a habit of giving. Look at a natural spring: animals come to drink there, trees and plants grow beside it, and humans build their homes nearby, because it keeps giving the pure water it receives from the summit to one and all. The spring teaches us that the only one true method for creating and sustaining life is to give, give what is best in our heart and soul. It is by becoming a spring that we obtain true wealth. We only truly possess what we are able to give.

11 May

*I*t is difficult to free ourselves from the astral and mental planes – ordinary feelings and thoughts – to rise to the causal plane where the spirit dictates its law. Just as a fish that decides to leave the sea or the river to step out into the open air should prepare its lungs, someone who wants to launch themselves up to the causal plane needs to develop the appropriate organs. And even when they succeed in projecting themselves up there, they cannot stay for more than a moment: they still lack the inner conditions required to remain there for any length of time.

You will one day be able to achieve these conditions if, through prayer and meditation, you strive to ascend to the higher regions of your being as often as possible. Little by little, you will feel the impact of this work upon your thoughts, your feelings, your daily behaviour, and even upon your health. It will be as if orders had been given from above to organise and harmonise everything within you. Imagine you are preparing to climb a mountain. This image will bring you to another mountain within you, and then another, until the day you reach the summit, the causal plane, your higher self.

12 May

***T**o live life eternal… This eternal life to which mystics aspire is not a length of time but a state of consciousness. From the moment we come into contact with the divine Source, and for as long as we dwell within it, eternal life begins to circulate within us. For eternal life is an abundant, rich and full quality of life.

A very simple image can give you an idea. Let's take a stick – it is a straight object with a beginning and an end, so something limited. Just like time. But now suppose that this stick is flexible and that it bends until the two ends meet: it becomes a circle, and this circle can give us an idea of eternity, with no beginning and no end, an infinite unit. Each moment of our life that we manage to link to the divine Source enters into the circle and becomes eternal life; on entering the circle, it changes nature, it is no longer a detached part of the Whole. While every point on the straight line is a moment of time, every point on the circle is a moment of eternity.

13 May

*S*uppose you wanted to reach the sun in a cart pulled by oxen – assuming there is a proper road from here to the sun for your oxen – how many thousands of years would it take you? If you were to go by boat on the cosmic ocean, it would take you almost as much time. If you were to take the train, you would get there faster. If you were to take a plane, you would arrive even sooner. And if you were to travel at the speed of light, you would arrive in eight minutes and a few seconds.

What do these examples mean? That someone who travels in an ox cart, that is, who only uses the physical body's means, the old methods to solve all problems, will only discover the truth thousands of years later. For someone who travels on water, that is, who walks at the speed of ordinary feelings, it will take almost as long. Someone who travels by air, who, in other words, uses their intellect, will go faster. But someone who can travel via the spirit and intuition, moves at the speed of light and discovers the truth immediately.

14 May

Christianity teaches the mystery of one God as three persons, which it calls the mystery of the Holy Trinity: the Father, the Son and the Holy Spirit. But for those who know how to apply the law of analogy, it is no mystery. One of these analogies is given to us by the sun.

The sun is a tremendous life-giving power that manifests itself through light and heat. When we delve more deeply into these manifestations, we discover the relationships that exist between the sun's life, light and heat, and the three persons of the Trinity. At every level of creation, from the physical plane to the divine plane, we find these three principles. On the spiritual plane, life, that is to say the almighty power of creation, manifests itself as wisdom or light, and as love or heat. These are the three principles found in the Holy Trinity – the Father, the Son and the Holy Spirit – which are inseparable just as the sun's life, light and heat are inseparable. The mystery of a God as three persons is therefore not that difficult to solve. What only remains mysterious is the immensity and the splendour of this primordial Essence from which all life arises.

15 May

*A*ll sorts of dark entities try to seduce humans. They must know how to recognize them and how to respond. To answer them, they can simply say 'no'.

Human beings' true power lies in saying no. No one in the world can make them do something they do not want to. Not even God can force them. If humans knew where their true power lay, they would triumph over every seduction, every temptation. If they make mistakes, it is because they consent to them. Evil spirits have the right and the means to tempt them, but they have no right to force them. It is through ignorance of their divine origin that humans succumb to the onslaught of evil. When they are able to say 'no', the spirits of darkness leave them and the spirits of light come to serve them. Each time they win an inner battle, each time they resist temptation, they receive light and strength.

16 May

Human beings are master of their destiny. Too many people still believe that their life is governed by chance or by fate; or that there is a superior will imposed upon them, the will of God or of the gods. To this day, the Church teaches Christians that their destiny is ruled by God's will, a mysterious, impenetrable will. When a child is born handicapped, a man unjustly condemned, or when a woman dies after being run over by a drunk driver while she crossed the street, someone might say, 'It is God's will'. No, there is no will of God that randomly distributes misfortune or happiness. For humans themselves, through the life they led in the recent or distant past, have prepared the conditions of their present life.

What we call destiny is but the fulfilment or the application of laws that people have themselves set in motion through their thoughts, feelings and actions. It is they who forge their destiny. If they have done wrong in the past, but henceforth decide to practice justice and righteousness, they will live a true life, the life of the soul and the spirit, immortal life.

17 May

Humans seek power, wealth, knowledge, love, and so on. But above all else, it is life they must seek. You may say you do not need to search for life since you have it, and that you must search for what you do not have. While it is true that you are alive, life is not the same in all beings, it has degrees.

Everything that exists is alive, from minerals to God, including plants, animals, humans and the angelic hierarchies. But being alive is not enough – we must ask ourselves what the quality of this life is. Of course, by virtue of their physical conformation, human beings lead the life of a human. But internally, their life can take on all kinds of aspects: that of stones, plants or animals, just as that of angels and archangels. It is this angelic life they must seek to make flow within them – this current that springs pure and clear from the original Source.

18 May

*P*roud people imagine they are great, and always see themselves rising above others. But in reality, they themselves are not growing, a tumour is developing inside of them. To inflate themselves is not the same as growing. A person's true growth causes rays, sparks, and vibrations beneficial to everyone to spring forth from them, and only humility fosters this growth.

One of life's great secrets thus lies in this so rarely understood and appreciated virtue: humility – the awareness that there exists a superior world and the will to be in harmony with the entities that inhabit it: the angels, archangels, and so on, up to God. This is why it can be said that humility is a form of intelligence. By casting their gaze upwards, a humble person discovers the infinity of heaven and feels drawn to it, absorbed by it. By simply changing the direction of their gaze, they enter into immensity.

19 May

What is a quality, a virtue? A spiritual being that has come to dwell in humans to manifest itself through them. So, if you want higher beings to come manifest themselves through you, by giving you new light and new powers, prepare the right conditions for them. And above all, show them that you have been able to bear fruit with what you have already received. Then, how joyfully they will go about enriching and embellishing you further, embellishing and enriching others through you too!

You will make these gifts and virtues bear fruit by participating consciously and harmoniously in universal life. And do not say this requires too much effort which others might not recognize. Whether others recognize your efforts or not should be of no concern to you. The only opinion that should matter to you is that of your heavenly Father; for it is to him that you will one day be accountable for the use you have made of the riches he has given you. As he has given them to you, they are yours, but they will only really belong to you if you make them bear fruit for the good of all.

20 May

Matter never ceases to oppose the spirit within us. Even when, after much effort, we succeed in dominating it, this victory does not last and we must continually start over again. And when I speak here of matter, it is not only about physical matter, but also about our psychic matter which resists us too. One moment, we succeed in getting it to obey, making it vibrate in unison with the world of light; the next moment, it returns to its initial inertia, and we must get back to work: meditating, praying, doing exercises. Obviously, we are able to master it little by little, but in order to maintain this control we must continue practicing tirelessly.

Even if a virtuoso musician has successfully developed their exceptional gifts, regardless of the level they have attained, they must practice for several hours a day in order to retain mastery of their instrument and be able to express through it the most subtle movements of their soul. It is the same in spiritual life: every day we must strive to subject our psychic matter to the power of the spirit.

21 May

When you take a walk in the forest, don't just look at the trees absent-mindedly as you go by, rather tell yourself that these are creatures through which you can regenerate yourself. Choose one: an oak tree, a pine tree, a beech tree, a birch, and so on. Greet it, asking it to give you some of its strength. Then lean back against it, placing your left hand behind your back, palm against the tree trunk, and the palm of your right hand on your solar plexus. Concentrate on thinking that you are receiving streams of life from this tree through your left hand, and that you are pouring them into your solar plexus with your right hand. After a few minutes you will feel at peace and strengthened. Then thank the tree for what it has given you, and continue on your way.

To practice this transfusion of energy properly, you must of course be aware that trees are living beings, and love them. These days, very few people have an idea of the tremendous strength the trees in the forest possess. Most people have lost the secrets of regeneration because they do not seek to study the language of each thing in nature. By learning to vitalize themselves with trees, people will rediscover these secrets.

22 May

You have all of eternity to explore the wealth of riches the Creator has placed within you. Do not look elsewhere, for they are all within you. Each and every day, you must dig, delve and seek to discover them.

Unless you search within, even if you were magically transported to a place in paradise, you would continue to wander starving, parched, and helpless. But if you have begun to discover paradise within you, wherever you go, whatever the conditions, nothing can drive you out. The outside world will certainly not have changed and you will encounter the same difficulties, the same ugliness, but because of the changes wrought within you, you will live increasingly in peace, beauty and light.

23 *May*

No human being, however elevated they may be, can come in direct contact with God. For God is an energy of such power that they would be instantly pulverised. There must always be an intermediary between the Divine and human beings, and the angelic orders are these intermediaries: they transform and filter this power in such a way for it to reach humans without obliterating them.

Even though it is said in the Bible that God spoke to the patriarchs and the prophets, it was not in fact he who spoke to them, but a messenger – which is exactly what the word 'angel' means. And even the word 'spoke' is inaccurate here. An angel does not speak in the sense that to speak means to pronounce words; but its presence, through the power of its vibrations, brings enlightenment, an inner direction, it inspires a project that the prophet translates into words.

24 May

*I*f you were in the habit of observing your hands, you would see that the lines which cross them – especially the life line, the heart line and the head line, which are the most important ones – can be paler or darker, and more or less pronounced. These differences reveal the state of your body, for all vital processes are written in the hands. This will become clear to you when you study how nature works on the physical body with the powers of electricity and magnetism, light and heat.

Hands constantly teach humans and make predictions for them. If humans knew how to interpret the signs, they would not venture lightly down dead ends. They read entire libraries, but they forget that they own one, the largest in the world, which they carry with them everywhere. This is also where the Creator has inscribed the mysteries of life: in their hands.

25 May

*L*ike all matter, that of our physical body is subject to time, and it wears out. This is what we call growing old, and we all grow old, which, of course, is not particularly pleasant. But we are not just a physical body, and if the wear of the body is in the natural order of things, internally, nothing forces us to grow old with it. Therefore, instead of becoming upset about the physical manifestations of age, humans should be concerned with nurturing that which always keeps them young and alive: their heart.

It is their heart, their capacity to love, not their body, that makes humans young or old, and if their heart ages, it is because they allow it to. How so? By losing their love for people and things, by losing their curiosity and their interest for the life that abounds all around them, the rich and abundant life of the universe. But if they strive to feel this life, if they seek to participate in it, to introduce it into themselves, they will not grow old.

26 *May*

When you open your eyes in the morning, what do you think about? The worries from the day before, the difficulties that await you, the problems you will have to tend to and so forth. This is not a good way to start the day. Set aside your worries till later, they can wait. Start by directing your thoughts towards heaven saying, 'Lord, I am thankful to be alive today. It is a new day – one for me to see, hear, walk, love and study. Strengthen my will so that everything I undertake may be in the service of good.'

Someone who expresses their gratitude to the Creator the moment they awake increases their inner love and light, and this love and light influence every moment of their day. They see the world around them with different eyes, they have a better attitude towards the people they meet, who open up to them because they feel the peace and joy they radiate.

27 May

*T*he universe is a body that God animates with his spirit. This is what the ancient philosophers called the macrocosm. Similarly, humans have a body, a microcosm, created in the image of the macrocosm, and the spirit that animates this body is a spark from the Divine Spirit.

For so many centuries it has been said that God created humans in his image! Which means that in creating us, he placed within us a quintessence of himself, of the same light, of the same purity, and of the same power. It is this divine quintessence within us that Initiatic Science calls the higher self. So, if we focus on our higher self, we connect with God, because our higher self is a particle of him. As a result of the efforts we make to reach this centre in ourselves – we can also say this summit, as from a spiritual viewpoint the summit corresponds to the centre – we bring forth forces that vivify all the cells of our body.

28 May

When we receive the word of a wise man, of a spiritual Master, we must consider it as a seed to plant in the ground. Once we sow it in our spiritual soil, we can watch it grow, we can feel a new life being born and developing within us.

If, for many faithful, religion is but a practice devoid of any meaning, it is because they do not know how to work with the words of truth that it presents to them. But let them sow these words in their inner earth as one sows seeds, and let them tend to them every day, keeping watch over them, watering them, keeping them warm. Let them clear away all the weeds threatening to choke them, let them get rid of the bugs about to nibble at them, that is to say let them prevent the thoughts and feelings inspired by their lower nature from coming to attack them: they will then feel a new life growing and developing within them.

29 May

*A*fter the flood, once the waters had receded, God said to Noah and his sons, *'Be fruitful, multiply and fill the earth.'* Do these words strictly mean that to obey God, humans must reproduce? In reality, we can attribute a broader meaning to them: give birth to children with a heart full of love and a luminous intellect, this is how you will expand your power on earth. What earth? Your own earth, yourself – through your feelings and your thoughts you will cover it with a magnificent generation.

When parents have a very intelligent and capable child, who excels in the sciences, the arts, politics, and so on, their influence begins to spread everywhere. This is also a way for parents to populate the earth: they populate it through their children and the successes they achieve. Similarly, all those who live in love and wisdom populate the whole world with bright thoughts and warm feelings: these children spread good seeds everywhere and improve the lot of all humans.

30 May

***P**eace, true peace is a stable and constant inner state. Once you have really achieved it, you cannot no longer lose it. It follows you everywhere. You may say that life is but a series of ups and downs: successes and failures, abundance and poverty, health and illness, joy and sadness, and so on – it is impossible to always feel at peace. Yes, once you have learned to re-establish, day in and day out, the bond between your consciousness and the spiritual centres located in your brain and your solar plexus, nothing will ever really trouble you. You could fall sick, suddenly lose your entire fortune, be imprisoned, persecuted, see your loved ones disappear, if you are solidly tethered to a fixed point within you, this peace will never leave you.

I am not saying you will not suffer anymore. But suffering does not mean losing one's peace. Insofar as your consciousness does not stagnate at the level of events, for each difficulty or hardship, you find an explanation or a truth that soothes and comforts you. Because you have managed to project yourself up to a very high summit, you understand that your difficulties and your suffering are fleeting, that you, yourself are immortal, and that there is a region within you where evil can no longer reach you.

31 May

***T**ake an object and give it your love. Say to it, 'There, I am placing you here where you will purify the air and sing.'

You have no doubt read that in ancient Egypt, the priests prepared objects that they placed inside the tombs in order to help the deceased in the afterlife. They used special techniques to do so, pronounced certain formulas. Even without knowing these formulas, you can already start to work with objects. And because you will regard them as living beings, you will also better understand the stories that are told about icons and statues that waved, bowed, spoke, smiled or cried. Even if you do not see them move, even if you do not hear them speak, a real link will be established between you and these objects. They will support you in your efforts to create a new world, they will accompany you on the path of light.

1 June

*I*nitiatic Science teaches us that before reaching the bright and clear regions of the causal or higher mental plane, the disciple must cross through the murky regions of the astral and lower mental planes. These regions are like patches of fog and dust. The fog is produced by excessive moisture of the heart: emotionality, sentimentality, greed and envy. As for the dust, it is produced by the practices and speculations of the intellect which only seeks out its own interests. And dust, like fog, prevents us from seeing things clearly.

Not only does an initiatic teaching instruct humans about the existence of the different worlds, it provides them with the criteria to discern the quality of their states of consciousness, as well as methods for crossing through the zone of illusory perceptions to reach reality. By virtue of work and exercise, the day is coming when the psychic world will appear to them with the same clarity, the same sharp focus as the physical plane.

2 *June*

*J*ust how many people forget the present and think only about the future! Since they are living in the present they don't really question themselves about it. Well yes, there are in fact questions to ask oneself. Tomorrow does not yet exist, and if we worry about it, it is a bit like throwing ourselves into nothingness. We must work on today, for today is here and it does not die – it will go on, and in prolonging itself, it will become tomorrow. You have yet to see, taste, or touch this tomorrow, it is not a reality. The moment you touch it, you will no longer call it tomorrow, but today, and what was today you will call yesterday.

The past is a memory and the future is a projection. Only the present is the true time of our life. Those who worry about the next day forget to live well in the present, and will therefore never know how this present can become an eternal present of harmony, beauty and light.

3 June

*O*ne often hears parents complain 'What did we do to deserve such a child?' Sadly, they did do something, if only being ignorant, for ignorance is the worst of misfortunes. And among the many aspects of this ignorance is the belief that the birth of a child is some kind of luck of the draw, a lottery.

Of course, many of a child's physical and psychic traits can be explained by heredity, but if this explanation were sufficient, children born to the same father and mother should not be so physically, morally and intellectually different. Yet it happens. This proves that there are other explanations – the laws of reincarnation, but also the nature of the elements and currents the parents attracted through their thoughts and feelings at the time of the child's conception. It is not enough to know about biology and physiology, one must know about the fluidic and energy processes that come into play both at the time of conception and during the pregnancy, in order to understand that there are forces there to channel towards a specific goal, a spiritual goal.

4 June

*W*e cannot comprehend what life is based on the phenomena we see in the physical world, for they only represent a part of it, an aspect of it. However, as they are the only ones directly available to our five senses, we must look to them to reflect on the more subtle, vaster, more universal realities.

All the spiritual traditions take mountains, trees and rivers as particularly rich and meaningful symbols. Why? Because from time immemorial, humans have seen in them a representation of cosmic life. Mountains, trees and rivers connect the world below to the world above. But whereas the mountain and the tree rise towards the heights, the river, whose source is in the mountain, descends and ends up joining the sea, a symbol of the depths. All life on earth comes from the sea and will one day return to the sea.

5 *June*

***H**ow many of the faithful ask to receive light and help from the angels only to be found looking elsewhere or dozing when the light and the angels appear? They then complain that praying offers them no support. Indeed, what support can those whose consciousness is slumbering receive? It is useless to pray to heaven if we have not first developed the faculties that will allow us to receive its answers and help. These faculties are foremost attentiveness and vigilance; they can be compared to a highly sensitive device that alerts us when our prayers are about to be answered. So, instead of bothering the Lord and his angels with requests, it is preferable to activate this device which will vibrate at their approach, announcing the arrival of a messenger, a visitor.

A true spiritualist knows that they must always be ready. Day after day, they seek to develop their receptive devices, they fine-tune their sensitivity, and because they remain vigilant, they hope not to be absent, deaf or blind when heaven opens up, when the Spirit comes to enlighten them.

6 June

Humans are rarely aware of their mental habits. When one person starts a job, they might be immediately stressed and tense; another person's first reaction when faced with any new situation might be to oppose it or to be critical; another person might feel too weak, and yet another may become quickly discouraged, and so on. But as they are not even aware of their reactions, they can do nothing to address them, and in any given situation, they always find an excuse to adopt a negative attitude.

So, the first thing that everyone must do is to study themselves in order to get to know themselves better. The moment they see themselves clearly, they will already have the means to remedy the situation: they will instantly receive a boost and be able to mobilize the possibilities the Creator has placed in their subconscious, their consciousness and their superconsciousness. By developing this habit of studying and being lucid about themselves, they will make progress each and every day.

7 June

*E*ven if you do not sense it very clearly, you are linked to the members of your family and of society, and as you make progress, all the riches and light you receive reflect upon them. As a result of your progress, they move forward too. And the same holds true if you begin to take a bad turn: all those to whom you are linked suffer harmful influences because of you. So, you are guilty twice over.

Everyone is responsible for their own actions not only with respect to themselves, but with respect to others. Do you wish to be useful and to help the whole of humanity, and even animals, plants, and all of nature? Take the path that leads upwards. Imperceptibly, you lead all of creation toward the heights, and the invisible world rewards you because through your conduct, you bring blessings to all beings. But be careful not to drag them down!

8 June

Our teaching presents you with exercises for every moment of the day. Obviously, you cannot do them all, but pick at least a few and practice them every day. These exercises will bring many improvements to your life, but most importantly, they will help you to develop your willpower. It is thanks to willpower that we overcome resistance and triumph over obstacles. Without exercise, it is impossible to develop our will.

There are many things we can receive from the exterior: wealth, knowledge, sensations, and so forth. But nobody can give us willpower, we must develop it ourselves. That is why a spiritual teaching first requires the disciple to exercise their willpower through discipline and regular activity. Of course this is hard, but it is what is most effective. Through willpower, you work, you insist, and in the end you get what you desire: light, love, power, health, beauty, and so on. Without willpower, no matter what you have, you will obtain nothing more, and you may even lose what you do have.

9 June

*T*he Holy Spirit descending upon the human soul is a symbol that can be found in all spiritual traditions in one form or another. But even if it is said that the Holy Spirit 'descends' upon humans, it is not an entity external to them: it is their higher self, this divine quintessence placed within them by the Creator, manifesting itself. Saying that humans receive the Holy Spirit means that they have managed to connect with their own spirit, their higher self. Like a drop of water in the ocean, like a spark in the fire, their higher self is made of the same quintessence as the Divine.

No event in a human being's life, no happiness, no grace can compare to this moment when they come into contact with the Holy Spirit. It is like a heavenly lightning bolt. However, it is not because they have received this bolt of lightning that they suddenly possess all virtues. The road to perfection is open to them, but they will still have to work a long time before reaching the goal.

10 June

*T*he ultimate goal of initiation is to receive divine fire. Those who have received this fire can wish for nothing beyond it. But much time and effort is required before this fire agrees to descend. For it can only enter into a dwelling especially prepared to receive it – a home that is purified and sanctified.

Every day, through meditation and prayer, but also through our feelings, thoughts and actions, we must build within ourselves a dwelling made of the most luminous materials, so that the fire, this divine guest, recognizing in it its own quintessence, is irresistibly drawn to it. And this divine guest does not come alone, it arrives with many servants: angels as well as nature spirits come to live in this person in the form of gifts, qualities, and virtues. Their outward appearance may not have changed, but within, everything will be transformed.

11 June

*S*omeone who gives their points of view claiming to speak the truth without first having worked hard on their inner self, not only runs the risk of being mistaken, but of misleading others too. They may be sincere, but they will not be right. Sincerity is one thing, and the truth is another. One can be sincere while wading through the worst mistakes, but one must never use the pretext of being sincere to justify oneself.

Those who sincerely seek the truth have only simple questions to ask themselves: Are my feelings inspired by true love? Do my thoughts follow the path of wisdom? Each time you include elements of wisdom and love in your thoughts and feelings, you get closer to the truth, you touch on a new aspect and reach a new level of it, and these aspects and levels are infinite in number. You must have found the truth and yet at the same time continue to seek it; that is to say, adhere to the two immutable principles of love and wisdom, while at the same time mobilizing all the resources of your will to embody these two principles in your life.

12 June

*G*od is always present in his creation, he continually supports it with his life and his love. And, at whatever level they may be, every human being can also participate in this divine work by striving to make the currents flowing in and around them converge toward the Source of life.

Think about this in the morning when you attend the sunrise. Look at the sun, realizing that it never stops illuminating, warming and vivifying all creatures. It is the best symbol of the harmonization and purification work we must all do, and this work has beneficial consequences not only for us, but for the whole world. At first, you may not understand the importance of it, because it takes a lot of time and effort for the events that take place in the subtle regions of your being to reach your consciousness. But even if you do not yet realize what effects your participation in this work produces, this participation is very real.

13 June

*I*n order to put the soul and the spirit first, certain religious leaders thought it would be good – especially during the Middle Ages – to encourage Christians to neglect their physical body, to loathe it, or even to mistreat it, of the view that not only has it no role to play in spiritual life, but that it even poses an obstacle. For Initiatic Science, this is a serious mistake; it is not good to separate the physical body from the soul and the spirit. By doing exercises to awaken the subtle centres located in different areas of the physical body, those who live by the rules of love and wisdom are able to gain a higher understanding of things.

As such, the Hindus are right in associating their three great deities, Brahma, Vishnu and Shiva, with the three vital centres of the physical body: Brahma, the creator, with the solar plexus; Vishnu, the preserver, with the heart; and Shiva, the destroyer, with the brain. Thus, Brahma, the creator, dwells in the solar plexus. Of course, physical life is perpetuated by the genitals, but humans enter into contact with the river of cosmic life through their solar plexus. When their solar plexus opens to the water of divine life, they themselves become a spring, and the water that irrigates their whole being also quenches the creatures that draw near to them.

14 June

*I*t is the nature of the astral body, the body of human beings' desires, to be insatiable: it constantly pushes people to desire ever more, even if it is to the detriment of others, and even if they have much more than they need. When the astral body is not disciplined or educated, it takes on inordinate proportions: money, objects, land, buildings, businesses, and so on – nothing escapes its greed. And as people endlessly give in to their desires, this astral body within them becomes something monstrous, a veritable tumour.

Human appetites can also be of another sort: ambition, sensuality, and so on. In some people, the astral body resembles a stomach whose hunger nothing can appease, a bottomless pit ready to suck everything in. These are the beings Jesus says in the Gospel will not enter the kingdom of God. For in God's kingdom, only beings capable of selflessness, of disinterestedness, of sacrifice are accepted – those who have learned to control their astral body.

15 June

So many people of faith beg the Lord to do away with evil spirits. But the Lord does not grant them their wish, because evil spirits are doing their job, they are authorized to tempt and mistreat them. It is up to the faithful to become more enlightened and stronger in order to avoid falling into their traps. Do you believe that it is the angels, the spirits of light, who are charged with putting humans to the test or going after them when they have done wrong? They have lots of other work to do! These thankless tasks are left to the spirits of inferior rank; it is they who are in charge of getting humans back onto the right track or making them suffer so that they may be strengthened by these difficulties. Since these spirits are servants, God will not eradicate them. Does a master exterminate his servants?

It is impossible to have a true idea about the question of evil if we do not start by admitting that the one we call Satan, the devil, or by whatever other name, is in fact in God's service.

16 June

Humans are like seeds thrown into the world by the Creator. Each seed carries within it the image of divine perfection and its predestination is to sprout and grow until it becomes a tree. While it is already wonderful to be a seed, it is even more desirable to become a tree with roots, a trunk, branches, leaves, flowers and fruit that will in turn produce seeds.

By striving to gradually improve each of our manifestations, we come closer to the perfection our heavenly Father has in mind for us. We bear the imprint of this perfection engraved for all eternity on our soul, and if we learn to focus on it, one day, we too will become trees of life.

17 June

Pessimism is generally considered to be a form of lucidity and wisdom. Are we not surrounded by danger? Nature and humans too, pose a permanent threat, and everything will end badly; we must, therefore, be wary and take precautions. The pessimist believes that by mistrusting everything, as evil can spring from anywhere, they are showing foresight. Well, no, this highly negative view of things is not foresight, and it is even harmful to the psyche.

Those who constantly think the worst will inevitably happen at any time and any place, end up with such a clouded outlook that they can no longer spot the dangers or the enemy when they actually appear; and moreover, they paralyze the vital forces within themselves that would enable them to react. So, where is the wisdom in that, since they lack lucidity and are depriving themselves of the means to face such situations?

18 June

*T*he moment people get married, they think they know what marriage is all about. No. Given the casualness and the obliviousness with which so many men and women decide to unite their destinies, they clearly do not. They do not know that before being a human institution, marriage is a cosmic phenomenon: the union of the two great masculine and feminine principles: God the Father, and his wife, the Divine Mother. Since man and woman were created in the image of these two principles, by marrying, they are simply repeating the mysteries that have been celebrated from the very beginning in the celestial regions.

Everything that exists in the universe is born of an encounter, a union, a fusion between the masculine principle – the spirit – and the feminine principle – matter. Marriage, its meaning, its greatness, comes from the fact that it is the reflection and the reiteration of cosmic phenomena.

19 June

If human beings' animal nature is so powerful, it is because for thousands of years, they had to face particularly difficult conditions in order to survive. Look at all the trouble animals go to in finding food, in seeking and maintaining shelter, raising their young, and protecting themselves from the attacks of other animals. It is the same for humans. After having lived in identical conditions, how can they now be good, generous, and open to others? So this is the issue each of us must now resolve: how to control this formidable instinctive force that lies within us? Not only is it present externally and collectively, it is also present within us.

So, tell yourself every day that you have nothing more important to do than to learn to master your lower nature with the weapons of the spirit. Otherwise, do you think it will be grateful to you for having fed and served it? Not at all! Greed and ingratitude are aspects of the lower nature. All those who have warmed and fed it always end up torn to pieces and devoured.

20 June

*W*e often hear people complain that they are lacking something. When will they become aware of everything they have received from God, their Creator? And they imagine they can justify their ingratitude by saying they do not believe in God. If they do not believe in God, they must think of everything they owe to nature: not only the elements of which their body is made, but also all that allows them to subsist: air, water, food, the light and heat of the sun...

Humans are often justifiably proud of their skills and ingenuity, but from where did they get the materials they use to make their instruments, devices and even their works of art? From nature. Yet, not only are they ungrateful, they spoil nature and waste its riches. In so doing, they transgress the laws of cosmic order symbolized by scales. For all that we receive, we must give something in return, at the very least our gratitude and respect. This is the balance of the cosmic scales.

21 June

*T*radition has it that when Orpheus played his lyre, he could charm humans and animals with his songs, indeed even plants, stones and the forces of nature. And in the Bible, it is said that it was to the sound of trumpets that the army of Israelites, led by Joshua, caused the walls of Jericho to fall. These stories, even of legend, cause us to reflect on the power of sound.

Whether from instruments or voices, sound vibrations act upon physical matter and psychic matter alike. This is why instrumental music and singing have played and continue to play such an important role in cultures and civilizations. They inspire emotions, provide impetus; they can even take hold of an entire being, as if their soul were torn from their body. Since time immemorial, humans have known how to use the power of sound, some to bring order and harmony to hearts and souls, others to introduce chaos and unleash passions. So strive to become aware of the effects that sound has upon you.

22 *June*

*T*he understanding of psychic disorders and the means to remedy them will remain limited until official science stops refusing to recognize the existence of invisible entities and reducing everything that transpires in people to physicochemical processes. Even if the reality of these physicochemical processes cannot be denied, we must understand that they are the consequence of psychic phenomena produced by living entities.

Obviously, biologists and surgeons should not expect to discover these entities through their microscopes or at the tips of their scalpels. However, our inability to see things or beings is hardly proof they do not exist. Have you ever seen germs and viruses? So, just as we open the door to germs if we allow impurities to enter our physical body, so too we open the door to dark entities that cause disorders by allowing impurities into our psychic body.

23 *June*

Before seeking to expand our wealth, our power and our conquests, each of us must strive to cultivate within ourselves a state of mind that allows us to appreciate what we already have, even if it is very little. For the essence is never in the possessions themselves, but in the feelings we get from the things we own.

It is our ability to experience feelings that makes us living beings, and as such, the slightest thing can satisfy us if we know how to consider it. Otherwise, we can possess a world empire and still feel poor and empty on the inside, because inside, we are dead. How can a dead person feel joy? To rejoice we have to be alive. And we are alive when we learn to refine our perceptions and develop a taste for things. And taste is often inversely proportional to quantity.

24 *June*

To justify their non-belief, some people say they will believe in God only when they see him. But the poor souls will never see anything, for no one has ever seen God. We can feel his presence, we can even see his manifestations – lightning, projections of light – but we cannot see the author of these manifestations, because it is simply impossible for physical eyes to see God.

For an object or being to be seen, it must have a shape, proportion, limits, and be situated somewhere in space or in time; however, God is beyond time and space. Therefore, we can only perceive reflections of him, manifestations scattered everywhere, among stones, plants, animals, and especially among humans: in their elevated thoughts, their feelings of generosity, their gestures of kindness or courage, and in their works of art. And the more we purify ourselves, the more we distinguish traces of God, of his life, his perfume and his music. When we contemplate the sun, we can say 'I saw God in the sun's light, I felt God in its warmth, and now, I am more alive.'

25 June

*O*ver the course of time, humans have acquired tremendous power over nature: little by little, they have managed to extend their dominion over the land, the seas, and now skyward. Their desire to explore the wide open space before them, and benefit from their discoveries is legitimate; what is not legitimate is the way they go about it. Just how far do they think they can go to conquer space without asking themselves if they are not in the process of upsetting a pre-established order, with all the consequences that will ensue for life on earth itself?

Humans will not be able to ignore for much longer the existence of the Intelligences that ensure the balance of the universe is not disturbed. These Intelligences do not appreciate the spirit of anarchy, the violence of certain researchers or those who help them to realize their projects in order to profit from their discoveries. They should not be surprised if one day, they are besieged by the forces of nature they recklessly unleashed.

26 June

*T*he goal of the work we do through our thoughts as we watch the morning sun rise and concentrate upon it, is to establish contact with our higher self. And here is a method that will help you.

As you gaze at the rising sun, imagine that you are already up there, in it, looking down upon yourself from above. Obviously, as you are down below on earth, you still feel very small, very limited; but from the moment that you are also up above in the sun, you build a bridge between yourself and your sublime self via thought. Then, gradually, the sun's light seeps into you, your consciousness broadens, you develop new faculties, and you are able to receive its revelations.

27 *June*

We say that some people are good, and that others are bad. But in truth, every human being is a mixture of both good and bad in different proportions. It is the good in each of us that urges us to examine ourselves in view of correcting and improving ourselves. And by improving ourselves, we change our destiny.

We all have the power to change the course of our destiny, to reverse the tides of fate, or to go against the current without being swept away, drowned, or cast onto the rocks. We must even learn to use the opposing force of the counter-currents to sail above all the obstacles, ride the wind and launch ourselves up to heaven. But only the spirit within us is able to achieve this marvel. When we associate ourselves with the spirit, when we unite with the spirit, we are no longer subject to destiny – we enter under the law of Providence, and Providence erases the old destiny. We were walking towards death, and now we are walking towards life.

28 June

***O**ur Heavenly Father sent us down to earth to work on the advent of his kingdom, and the beings of light in the invisible world constantly provide us with favourable conditions for this work. But because these conditions rarely present themselves as we expect them to, we are seldom aware of them. It is so easy to be deceived by appearances.

Many people who decide to undertake spiritual work expect Providence to grant them special favours and ideal conditions to make their task easier. And then, they encounter opposition and obstacles. Rather than complaining, becoming overwhelmed and giving up, they must study what is happening to them. What is the invisible world trying to tell them? What does it expect from them by sparing them neither difficulties nor failures? For despite appearances, difficulties and failures are also good conditions they must try to use to contribute to the realization of the kingdom of God within themselves and throughout the world.

29 June

*E*very human being is seemingly isolated and separate. In reality, there is a spiritual part of us that lives in the collective whole and in all beings, and we must become aware of this in order to feel fulfilled.

Sometimes, someone complains to me unhappily, saying, 'I am alone, I have no family'. In reality, they have a huge family, but their awareness is so limited, so obscured that they do not feel it. And this is the case for millions of people in the world: they feel alone, and yet... They must start to broaden their awareness, and they will understand that even if they no longer have a father or a mother, a brother or a sister, or any blood relatives, that is no reason to believe they are alone. In truth, they are all sons and daughters of the same Father, the cosmic Spirit, and the same Mother, universal nature. Let them work for all their brothers and sisters in the world, and they will never feel abandoned or unhappy again.

30 June

*W*hen you invite friends over, you know how to welcome them if you want them to feel comfortable in your home and for them to want to come again. Not only do you offer them your best food, you serve it on the best china you save for special occasions. If you know how to draw conclusions from this simple fact of everyday life, you will become more vigilant. The moment you are tempted to waste your inner riches, a sort of warning bell will go off, and you will do your best to hold on to them. You will sense that these are foods that you must save for celestial guests in order to attract them and make them stay.

Also tell yourself that, contrary to what goes on in human societies where distinguished guests usually only accept invitations from those who belong to the same social class, spiritual entities only consider souls. They immediately feel which are noble, beautiful and capable of welcoming them, and it is to them that they pay a visit. These entities see princes and princesses in the souls of those who have learnt to welcome and nourish them.

1 July

*W*ater is the earth's vital fluid. Like the blood circulating in our body, it is a precious and vital element that feeds all of nature's kingdoms. It is even required for the formation of crystals: precious stones exist only thanks to water particles without which they would turn to dust. Water makes stones resistant and gives them their colour and transparency.

Vegetation, with its roots sinking into the ground, forms the earth's etheric body which is sustained by water. Thanks to water, flowers, trees and all the plants give the earth form and life. Not only does water flow on the surface of the earth, it also has an underground network with which its emanations feed the different kingdoms of nature, like an elixir of life. Stones, plants, animals and humans exist due to the presence of water circulating in the bowels of the earth.

2 *July*

For as long as they are alive, criminals may remain indifferent and insensitive to what they inflict on others, and they may even succeed in escaping human justice. But when they die, they will not escape divine Justice. During their life on earth, their physical body, like a shell, prevents them from sensing the reality of the psychic world. But once they have been separated from their physical body, they are defenceless to their inner world, and the torments they fall prey to are nothing other than the consequences of the conditions they themselves created throughout their life.

Cosmic Intelligence does not seek to take revenge or to punish them; no, it simply has laws that everyone must learn to respect in order to improve themselves. If they transgress these laws, they must go through the same suffering they inflicted on others. This is the only way to make them aware of their acts and draw lessons for their next incarnation.

3 July

We receive so much from a simple inner movement of gratitude for the life we have been given. This movement of gratitude goes far beyond a mere feeling. The moment we intend to give thanks, this feeling of gratitude starts to act, it does not remain passive. According to the law of affinity, its vibrations attract impressions, feelings and inspirations of the same nature. We then receive all the blessings thanks to this one small movement: we thought to give thanks.

Someone might say, 'But I am unhappy, sick and poor, so I cannot thank.' Of course they can, for even if they are unhappy, if they think hard, they will find at least one reason to be grateful. Everyone must be grateful for what they have and for what they don't have, for what brings them joy and for what brings them sorrow. This is how they will keep the flame the life alive in them.

4 July

By simply glancing at the structure of a human body and the way it functions, we discover with what ingenuity and wisdom Cosmic Intelligence created it so that we may make it the spokesperson of our spirit. Our spirit and our body are not separate from each other. Our spirit's main role is to work on our body, and then, thanks to our body, to work on the entire earth, for the earth is, in a way, an extension of our own body.

Most human beings appear to have no idea what they are here in this world for. Yet, deep down within themselves they know; they know that they are here to use the power of their spirit to create. Cosmic Intelligence has etched this programme in them. But because they are caught up in the constraints of matter, they forget and they leave this life having destroyed more than they built; starting very precisely with their own body which, through their neglect and excess, they have been incapable of keeping in good health.

5 July

*G*od is infinite and vast, and he permeates the entire universe with his presence; each one of us is an infinitesimal part of Him. But so many people complain that God does not hear them or answer them. And they say that since he is deaf, why should they continue to turn to Him. Well no, God is not deaf, but these people have a shell so thick that his presence, light and love cannot reach them. All communication routes have been blocked by the layers of impurities they have formed with their thoughts, feelings and acts. If they work to purify themselves until their subtle bodies become receptive, the communication will one day be restored and the presence of the Divine will overwhelm them.

Just as God lives in us, we also live in God. When humans will be able to understand God in this way, they will experience his presence in them as life, energy and light that nothing can take away from them.

6 July

*N*obody would venture into the abysses of the earth or the depths of the seas without the right equipment or sufficient preparation and training. But when it comes to descending into the depths of their own nature, people think it is easy and without risk. However, that is where the greatest dangers lie, and to avoid them, you must prepare and equip yourselves by rising up to the regions situated above your consciousness and self-consciousness – to the regions of the super-consciousness.

Anyone wanting to explore the subconsciousness must first rise on high, because it is up there in the higher world that they will acquire knowledge about the lower worlds and the entities living there. They must also develop purity and self-control so as to form an aura of light around themselves to protect them and guide them in this dark labyrinth. The lower entities, sensing that they are well-armed, will move away. And if they find themselves in danger, the heavenly beings, who know that these humans have reached the end of their evolution and must therefore explore the abysses within themselves, will not abandon them.

7 July

*I*n the Emerald Tablet, Hermes Trismegistus reads a mysterious sentence: 'Its father is the sun and its mother the moon; the wind has borne it in its body, and the earth has nourished it.' With its light, the sun gives the seeds; the moon is the ether that reflects and sends back the light; the wind carries the seeds; and the earth: we must first nourish ourselves with the sun's rays to then in turn nourish them, just as a mother feeds her child. Because we must also give something of our own substance to the sun's rays so they may grow and develop in us.

Each morning we receive the sun's light, warmth and life, and we must preserve them, reinforce them and feed them until the following day so that they may go deep within us. Whether we are men or women, we are like a mother in whom a work of gestation takes place. Everyone one must support, help and nourish what the sun has entrusted to them.

8 July

When a project means a lot to you, if you wish to be well prepared and equipped to bring it to fruition, don't tell everyone about it beforehand. Start by putting it into action, for you will have plenty of time later to make it known it and comment on it. 'Why these precautions?' you might ask. Because there are dark entities around you and within you that are ready to put obstacles in your way using your family, friends, work colleagues and neighbours, and you will meet with great difficulties, or simply fail. Not to mention those who, apparently with the best of intentions, will try to discourage you by saying: 'But do you think it's worth the trouble?' Shouldn't you rather leave that for others to do?'

So, as far as possible, wait until some of your good plans have begun to be realized before you talk about them. Once they have started to take shape, they will be like a well-rooted tree that the winds cannot blow down. And this tree will yield fruit that you can share with those around you.

9 July

*T*hanks to scientific and technological progress, humanity has gained significant power over matter, and we can therefore say that the past century has surpassed all others before it. However, the material world now fascinates our contemporaries and has a hold on them to the point they lose sight of the realities of the spiritual world. Only their physical eyes are open and they seek whatever they can to satisfy their curiosity or their interests. It is as if their inner eye, the eye in the subtle regions of their being, is struck with blindness.

A good inner vision of things can only be acquired through purity. This is why our teaching stresses the importance of a pure life, on the physical plane and also on the psychic plane. Human beings' destiny depends on the clarity their inner eye, and this clarity in turn depends on their way of life. If they transgress divine laws, their spiritual vision clouds over and they can no longer be warned nor guided, and they get lost in dead ends. But if they decide to lead a clean life, with honesty and integrity, their subtle centres will start to function and they will be able to see, and also live in the light.

10 July

A true spiritual Master does not turn their back on sinners and criminals. Like a tree that transforms phloem sap from the xylem sap which rises from its roots, a spiritual Master draws energies from uncultivated and disinherited people and criminals and transforms and redistributes them in the form of purity, light and love. Beings of great purity know they can frequent all kinds of people and social groups without being afraid of being soiled by others. Their love is stronger than anything and it is this love that makes them capable of transforming humans. Therefore, contrary to what too many people believe, avoiding sinners and the weak is not a sign of evolution.

Obviously, love and the desire to help others do not suffice to tear people from their vices or weaknesses. How often have we seen generous people get drawn down as low as the very people they wanted to save? They had overestimated their strength. To transform others, you must first have learnt, patiently and over much time, to do this transformational work on yourselves.

11 July

*T*he number 6 represents animals and the number 5 represents human beings. When human beings stand with their arms and legs spread out, they fit in the shape of a five-pointed star, the pentagram. The 5 thus represents humans who have rid themselves of their animal nature which is symbolized by the tail; and they must bring the 5 alive in them by working with the five virtues of the pentagram: wisdom, love, truth, kindness and justice.

It requires great effort to evolve from an animal to a human, from the 6 to the 5, because human nature is still so close to the animal nature with all its instincts and appetites. We all drag our animal past along with us: cunningness, brutality, cruelty, voracity and sensuality, and we will never be able to rid ourselves of it completely. But each one of us can seek to control all these instinctive tendencies by developing our spiritual faculties that will truly make us humans.

12 July

*I*mmutable laws govern the universe created by God and make it work. As such, human beings who are part of this universe must always study these laws and seek to better understand them and abide by them. They suffer due to the difficulties they encounter on their path; but these difficulties are also a source of riches for them because they make them surpass themselves.

One may often wonder why the Lord does not spare the righteous. Because he loves them. His love brings them growth and fulfilment; they simply need to ask themselves how they can use their suffering to improve themselves. You must not seek suffering of course, but when it appears, do not try to escape it, for through suffering you progress. And there is always progress to be made so you may go further and rise higher.

13 July

*A*ll spoken words are like a rocket travelling through space and on its way it releases forces and awakens entities. If you regret having spoken badly about someone, make amends by saying something nice about them. But hurry, because the more time passes, the less your good words will have the power to neutralize your negative ones: for since you said them later, they have been recorded in a different layer of the atmosphere and the layers are superimposed.

There is a means that is still more powerful than speech: that of thought. But another problem arises: thought and speech belong to two different planes. Speech belongs to the physical plane, like a wave that moves through the air; while thought belongs to the etheric plane. But try all the same. If you have unknowingly said some unfair or unkind words about someone, when you realize you have done so, try to connect with the benevolent entities of the invisible world and, by means of thought, send this person much light and love. Some damage might have already been done and it will take time before they feel the effects of your good thoughts, but you will have avoided the worst.

14 July

Many people say they have found meaning in their lives thanks to love, others thanks to power, study or to life's pleasures. Yes, maybe. But in reality, human beings can only truly find the meaning of life in work – work dedicated to a divine goal. This work makes them beneficial to humanity, to the point that during their sleep, beings of light caring for our planet invite them to take part in their councils. Initiatic Science reveals the mysteries of human beings to us and teaches us about their spirits and souls and about the nature of their activities and powers.

Once you understand this, you will know that the only thing you can count on is this work that you have decided to undertake for your improvement and for the good of the entire world. The day you can truly place this work first, you will not be able to find the words to describe how you feel, for through this work you will feel true life flood your entire being.

15 July

*T*here is a warning sign to be seen in the fact that more and more people, especially the youth, are turning to drugs. It is the human soul trying to make its needs known: for it is suffocating and drugs are a means to free itself. Apparently, this 'opium' that is religion, was supposed to have been banished? Well, we now have marijuana, heroin, cocaine and so on. Is this preferable?

The soul needs the infinity of space. And when it feels limited and smothered, it seeks whatever means it can to free itself. Alcohol and drugs are examples of these means because they can push the soul out of the physical body and momentarily give it an illusion of freedom and space. But this is only an illusion because drugs are just a material element given to the body. And it is the soul that needs to free itself, not the body. Drugs are a clue that the soul seeks to travel in infinite space, but they cannot satisfy its needs. Not only are drugs unable to satisfy it, but they also destroy the physical body.

16 July

*L*ike chemists, alchemists work with an element they call 'salt'. But what they call salt and what they call mercury and sulphur have nothing in common with the chemical substances of the same name. Only the correspondences between them are the same: just as salt is the product of an acid and a base in chemistry, it is the product of sulphur and mercury in alchemy.

Sulphur must be seen as the masculine principle which manifests as our intellect and on the plane above, as our spirit; mercury represents the feminine principle, our heart and higher still, our soul. And salt, our will, represents the balance that should ideally reign between the two. Will is expressed through actions: through their actions, humans reveal the extent to which they have been able to create harmony between their intellect and their heart, and between their thoughts and feelings. Through their physical body, they express the wealth of their spirit and soul, of which their intellect and heart are the instruments. And by means of their physical body, the instrument of their will, humans must bring the Divine down on to the earth.

17 July

When people are criticized or insulted they might exclaim, 'I couldn't believe my ears! It made me sick.' There are words that can indeed be perceived as real poisons, but why let them enter you?

No words must make you lose your peace and light. You may say it is impossible not to be disturbed or hurt by certain negative remarks. When someone speaks to you, obviously you hear them; but inwardly you could very easily shut their words out. You don't have to take poisons in. So take care to prevent them from entering you; and if you were not able to, immediately try to neutralize them to make them easy to absorb. Take the example of a tree. What does it do when you put manure around its base? It carries out all the necessary secret transformations it knows, and in exchange for the disgusting and foul-smelling matter it receives, it produces beautiful, fragrant and delicious fruit.

18 July

*I*n order to understand the importance of the present day, we must act as if it were our last. Some may say it's awful to keep thinking of death in that way. Well, it isn't. Thinking of each day as if it were your last does not drive you towards death, but towards life. No, the ones walking towards death are those who behave in a superficial, careless way while continuing to hope for a better future. Yes, they are squandering their life. When the wise tell us we must live each day as if it was our last, they say it so we will do our best to make today more useful, more beautiful and more precious. It is not that you really believe it is your last day; you are merely using the idea as a teaching method for living today more fully.

You have a minute here, an hour there, a day perhaps. This minute, hour or day is yours to create your future. Before the future, your true future as the son or daughter of God, can appear in all its splendour, it waits for you to learn all your lessons from the past. But it is alive and moving, and it is already here since you are creating it.

19 July

*A*s you rid yourselves of your bad habits, the dark entities that had settled in you are obliged to leave you, because your inner atmosphere becomes unbreathable for them. Once exterior to you, they seek new homes in other people through whom they then try to harm you. But the damage is less great compared to when these entities squatted you, and since you were able to overcome them within you, you are stronger and better able to overcome them when they appear externally.

Even if confronting external enemies is often difficult, they are always less dangerous than your inner enemies who attack your soul. With respect to your external enemies, employ diplomacy and patience, but when it comes to your inner enemies, the dark entities you attracted, you must act with authority. Unfortunately, human beings often do the opposite: they are indulgent with their inner enemies, but are aggressive towards their external enemies. There is therefore no surprise they continue to struggle in such inextricable situations.

20 July

How can you be made to understand that the sun is so much more than just a star shining in the sky?

In the morning, when you see it appear and rise on the horizon, imagine that you rise with it. The vibrations of your entire being will gradually intensify. You will soon feel the sun enter you so deeply that you will no longer be able to distance yourself from it. Every element in your being will be exalted. You will feel projected into increasingly vast and luminous regions in space, you will discover truths that remained hidden to you up until now, and the notion of time will cease to exist. For a few moments at least, you will forget the earth with its tragedies and misery, and you will live in eternity.

21 July

*I*n Egypt, India, Thrace, Greece, Palestine, and so on, many places considered holy in the world have lost the spiritual power and the influence they had in the past. Over centuries, such places that had been marked with the imprint of exceptional beings have since been profaned by the presence of many people with impure thoughts and feelings and lacking in light. Whatever the holy nature of a place and the imprints inscribed everywhere on the walls and objects by beings of great spiritual elevation, everything is lost if such a place is exposed to the comings and goings of people without the appropriate attitude and who don't know how to maintain its holy nature: the heavenly beings that were living there have left.

You can of course visit 'holy places', but do so with the awareness that above all, they must lead you to finding the one true holy place, the one within you, in your soul. Once you have found it, wherever you go, you will commune with all the great spirits that have incarnated on earth and you will be nourished by their wisdom and love.

22 *July*

*I*n his dialogue *'the Banquet'*, Plato relates the myth of the androgyne. In the beginning, human beings had both male and female organs, they were all both male and female, and this double nature gave them capacities such that the gods ended up feeling threatened. To weaken them, Zeus, king of the gods, decided to cut them in half, and from then on there were men and there were women. This myth stresses that human beings' power came from the fact they had both male and female organs.

But despite this kind of mutilation, humans nevertheless possess the two principles physically. Yes, in their mouth: their tongue is the masculine principle, their two lips are the feminine principle, and together they create a child: speech. Speech gives them immense power. Sometimes, just a few words are needed to bring them the same results material means would. Through speech they create and destroy, gather together and separate, restore peace or trigger war, bring healing or disease. Each one of you must be aware and careful of the words you say.

23 July

*N*ature has a life with different manifestations that follow on from one another and bring changes. And there is above all the alternation of day and night. The sun governs the day and the moon the night, they are of equal importance and are also present in human beings. During the day, we are awake and active; at night, we sleep and rest, but this does not mean there is no activity. While we sleep at night, much organising and cleansing takes place in our body, and thanks to this cleansing, we wake up full of energy.

The work done during the night while we sleep is very important. Since it takes place in our subconsciousness, most humans know nothing of the processes taking place within them. But they can seek to become aware of them, and in the morning when they wake up, how grateful they will be to find they are on their feet once again, in good health, fully aware and alert.

24 July

A young boy who is very content with his family, friends and studies, might nevertheless get bored. But one day, he meets a girl who he falls in love with. And so everything changes: the world appears magnificent to him, alive with colour and music. In reality, nothing has changed; he has made an inner discovery: that of love which makes everything beautiful. Even if it rains, to him the sun is shining. But if this girl were to disappoint or betray him, his life would become dull and pointless again.

You may say you already know that. Well yes, but what have you learnt from this? For there is something to learn: this teaches you that, to find a taste for life, you must seek an element capable of transforming everything in you, one that no outside event can make you lose. You will not find this element in the love of a man or a woman, for that love is always uncertain. You must seek it very high up in the regions of the soul and the spirit.

25 *July*

*T*he words we say always express our thoughts, feelings and desires. These thoughts, feelings and desires first create kinds of diagrams and lines of force in the invisible, around which particles of matter arrange themselves according to the words we utter. This is why the spoken word plays an important role in their realization.

Take for example the image of a rifle. Our speech represents the barrel of the rifle; and our thoughts, desires and plans represent the gunpowder. The barrel directs, and the gunpowder gives power. To obtain results we must have powerful thoughts, feelings and desires, and then, through what we say, direct them in the way we desire. Psychic energy and speech both have a role to play, and it is wise to remember this in spiritual practice.

26 July

*W*anting to be in the service of the Lord is not enough to be capable of serving him. We must prepare ourselves, learn and practise. Just look at what happens in everyday life: would the first person who came along make a good employee, a good secretary or a good minister, simply because they sincerely wanted to be one? No, they must study first and acquire certain abilities and qualities. All the more so, then, when it comes to serving the Lord. What will someone do if they have not prepared themselves? They will make many mistakes. They will think they serve the Lord, when in reality, they are still serving their prejudices, biases and illusions.

Several times a day, turn to the heavenly beings and tell them you wish to serve them, ask them to inspire you and show you how to act. In this way, you will become a good servant of God and partake in the work of your Master.

27 *July*

*T*o fully understand the different manifestations of life, we must study them in the three planes – the physical, psychic and spiritual planes – that correspond to the division of body, soul and spirit. This division into three also applies to our physical body: our head symbolizes our spirit; our rib cage, our soul; and our stomach and belly, our body.

Our soul therefore corresponds to our rib cage, and our arms are included in this part too. The spirit enlightens, brings order and organizes, and it guides our soul which, through our arms and hands, works on matter. It is generally thought that the soul manifests through our eyes and the look in our eyes. This is true in the sense that our soul is revealed or expressed in our eyes, and that's what makes people say that eyes are the mirror of the soul. But for it to act, our soul needs our hands. If our hands possess magical powers, it is because they are the instrument of our soul.

28 July

A desert may at first appear to be empty and without life, and therefore seem to be of no interest or even sometimes dangerous, and people may think they must cross it in a hurry. However, deserts, like mountain summits, are in reality places that are far away from the noise, agitation and disorderliness of human beings, and they are alive and inhabited. Spirits of nature, and also certain very advanced beings that have now left the earth, go there to find a place of refuge where they are undisturbed in their work, and their presence can be felt there. In the silence of these vast stretches of land between earth and heaven, the soul feels it can return to the original Source where it can drink and eat.

Much work is required to detach oneself and to forego distractions and easy pleasures before being able to find spiritual nourishment in the desert. Only saints and initiates are capable of doing so, and in this silence which is alive and vibrates, their thought frees itself to undertake a true work of creation.

29 July

*W*hatever mistakes you make, nothing can prevent you from returning to the path of salvation if you really want to. And tell yourselves that heaven can have even greater trust in people who have understood the error of their ways and repented than in people who have never lost their way. Why? Because those who have never been lost are unaware of the precautions they must take: they are inexperienced and they don't see clearly, they can go anywhere blindly and one day, they will falter. But heaven will accept in its service those who have erred, suffered, learnt the lesson and are able to find the right path again, saying, 'At last, here is someone who can be relied on!' Whatever your falls, it is always possible to get up again.

But these words of encouragement must not be a pretext to let yourselves go and think you have plenty of time to get back on the right path. No, for heaven does not appreciate careless people. You have all committed enough errors in the past. Instead, think about how you might benefit from the good conditions you are given by the light of a spiritual teaching.

30 July

***H**ow* often do the heart and the intellect give opinions like measuring and weighing instruments that are broken or out of order. This is why human beings make so many errors of judgement and behave inappropriately. They transgress divine laws, and in so doing not only do they hurt themselves, they also hurt others. This is why they don't understand each other and continually confront one another.

However, humans are not condemned to fight like this forever. God created them so they could get along and live together in harmony. A summit is present within them – their higher self – and they must strive towards it every day to learn the universal language of love, wisdom and truth. When they agree to learn this language, they will begin to understand the language of God and they will also understand each other.

31 July

*I*f human beings feel no need to link themselves to the divine world, they deprive themselves of something precious. Of course, those who are intelligent, determined and in good health can, for a certain time, have the impression they still possess all their faculties. But as they are not being fed by currents from above and don't receive new energy, something in them gradually begins to crumble. They leave the door open to undesirable entities that will eat away at their heart and mind like worms gnawing at wood. The ignorant dwell on temporary situations and draw conclusions from them, saying, 'Link with the divine world? But why? I know so many people for whom the divine world doesn't exist and yet they are very successful.' Yes, but until when?

God must come first in our life and we must give him our love, for this love brings us everything: wisdom, power, freedom, beauty, good health... and also love of course. God does not need our love, but we need to love him, because in loving him we open ourselves to him and we receive his love in return.

1 August

*W*hy deceive people by preaching that all they need to do to be saved is have faith? Faith is only a requirement, a starting point. Then they have to set to work so that the forces of the universe have a reason to get moving. Those who are content to say, 'I believe, I believe', without giving more concrete expression to what they believe, will always go hungry in some way or another. But if they sow just a few seeds – some thoughts, feelings and words inspired by disinterestedness, kindness and love – all the powers of heaven and earth, of rain and sun, will be at hand to make the seeds germinate and grow. One day, they will have a whole field from which to feed both themselves and a multitude of other creatures.

What you have to believe in to be saved is your own activity. For even the most insignificant activity is bound to produce results. So, make sure that every one of your thoughts, feelings and actions becomes like a seed sown in spiritual soil. Then the forces they set in motion will benefit you and the whole world.

2 *August*

People are rarely aware that fire puts them in touch with and activates primordial powers. Nor do they understand what fire represents on the psychic plane. We can say that on the psychic plane there are two sorts of fire: the astral fire of lower desires, which consumes beings, forcing them to endure great suffering, and the fire of spiritual aspirations, which allows all that is pure and noble in them to shine. How many know the astral fire of lusts and sensual passions, which plunge them into a living hell! With what pleasure this fire leaps upon them and devours them, as they have everything it needs to feed on, and soon all that is left is ashes and smoke.

Spiritual fire, on the other hand, seeks out those who walk the path of disinterested love, self-denial and sacrifice. This fire has the property of never destroying anything of the same nature as itself. When it enters someone, it burns only those few impurities that remain in them. The pure matter of their being is not consumed and itself becomes light, because it has the same vibration as divine fire.

3 August

The symbol of a triangle with a central eye is very widespread in Christianity and certain spiritual movements. According to tradition, it represents the all-seeing eye of God. But that does not mean, as some naively believe, that God spends his time watching humans and noting all their good and bad actions so that he can reward or punish them. This eye of God is really within us, and those who are able to sense this eye watching them will progress without the risk of going astray.

Whether our inner eye is open or closed depends on us. Indian yogis call it the third eye and say it is just above the nose. In the chakra system it corresponds to the ajna chakra. Our physical eyes form a triangle or, rather, a prism with the third eye. When a beam of light passes through the surfaces of a prism, it breaks up into seven colours. In the same way, when a beam of spiritual light hits our third eye, it breaks up into just as many colours, which strengthen our aura, making it sensitive to the realities of the soul and spirit.

4 August

*T*he Creator gave humans a mission: to bring the spirit down to dwell in them, so that everything in them that was lifeless would be brought to life. They have great obstacles to overcome before they achieve this, but that is their work: to awaken the powers the Creator has placed in them, so that they can fully realize their divine predestination.

So, from now on, everyone knows what they have to do; they just have to be willing to do it. Lazy people will claim they are not clear what spiritual work is, but they are not being honest with themselves, that's all. Those who truly want to work will receive the necessary teaching and advice; if they refuse it, they will suffer. Of course, those who undertake this work will suffer too – as long as we are on earth, we cannot fail to suffer – but it is not the same kind of suffering. And they accept it, because it feels as though this suffering becomes a blessing for them: they learn how to use it to grow in the light.

5 August

*T*he disciples of a spiritual teaching are aware that within them there is something beautiful and great that longs only to express itself, and they seek the help of beings of light from the invisible world. Their wish flows from them as a subtle fluid, and the entities that pick this up are always ready to respond to their request. But it is one thing to have a spiritual ideal and quite another to keep it firmly in your soul. When you have succeeded in elevating your inner state, it is difficult to stay on the high ground. But you have to cling on, because it is up there that you will find pure air, light and freedom.

In our universe, it is the sun that represents the summit, the spirit. In order to reach their inner summit and remain there, disciples of spiritual science must make daily efforts to hoist themselves up to the sun. Then when they come back down to face whatever events may occur, a part of them will remain up above, in the sun, inspiring all their decisions.

6 August

*H*umans are always ready to fight evil. Certainly, their intentions are good, but they will never succeed in conquering it, in society or in other people. And they will not conquer it in themselves either. You may say, 'But what must we do, then?' Deal only with what is good. In dealing only with what is good, we draw on the energies of evil, which we are then able to transform. Just like grafting.

What do gardeners do? Into the stem of an unproductive but sturdy tree, they insert a shoot from a good quality tree, which will benefit from the other's sturdiness. We have to do this same operation in our psychic life, since we are similar to trees. Thanks to the light of the spiritual sun, we can transform the raw sap of our instinctual tendencies into elaborated sap, which will then provide the flowers and fruits of our soul and our spirit.

7 August

*E*veryone should be careful what they say, because speech is a terrible weapon. At the level of actions, people are limited: it is not so easy to ruin someone, to destroy their career or to get rid of or annihilate their family. And, even if these things were possible, you would risk being arrested and convicted. But humans have speech, and they can hurl words on all sides without too much risk to themselves, and their words are like lit matches starting fires – in their family, in those around them, in their place of work, in society and sometimes even in the whole world.

So many break-ups and tragedies are caused by a few spoken or written words, deliberately used at a time when the user knows they will produce the most damage! And nowadays, what with the telephone, the press, radio, television and so on, there are so many possibilities for people to act with words! So, they must be more and more careful, because even if human justice closes its eyes, divine justice will judge them severely.

8 August

*A*sk humans what peace is: most will reply that it is being able to live quietly, away from disturbance or stress. No, peace is the consequence of the different principles that constitute our psychic make-up being in agreement: our spirit, soul, mind, heart and will.

If obtaining this agreement is so difficult, it is because everyone has particular needs they wish to satisfy. Some people's thoughts are lucid and wise, but passionate feelings have sidled into their heart making them lose all control. Others are full of the best intentions, but their will is paralysed. Or there are those whose soul and spirit long for retreat, but the world around them is so seductive that their heart and mind get carried away. How can they feel at peace in the middle of all this conflict? Those who understand that peace is a consequence, an outcome, are the only ones who will finally come to know it and make it their reality. They understand that it is a state of consciousness, in which all functions, all psychic activities, are in perfect balance and harmony.

9 August

*E*ach day we have to solve the problems posed by the fact that we have two natures, a higher and a lower nature, or our individuality and our personality. So, we must begin by acquiring the knowledge that will enable us to tell the difference between the two. And most importantly, if we do not want to be continually pulled this way and that between them, we must put our lower nature in the service of our higher nature and keep a constant eye on it, because it is rebellious and crafty. Even if it appears to accept the authority of the higher nature, it is in fact endlessly seeking to overturn its power.

Perhaps you think, then, that the simplest thing would be to get rid of the lower nature? No, it is part of being human; without it, humans would not be able to survive, because it is a store of hidden resources: their instincts, their appetites and everything that enables them to remain attached to the earth, where they are destined to live for a certain amount of time. They just have to learn to be more intelligent and stronger than it is, for once it is mastered it is their higher nature's best servant.

10 August

*M*ost religions have given God a human appearance, because they had to make the realities of the spiritual world accessible, and these realities go well beyond most believers' abilities to comprehend them! Smallness cannot comprehend immensity, the limited cannot comprehend the limitless, and the finite cannot comprehend the infinite. When will the small, limited and finite ever understand? When it enters the immensity, when it merges with it, when it becomes part of that life.

As long as a drop of water is separate from the ocean, it cannot know the ocean, even though its composition is identical. But if it returns to the ocean, it can no longer be separate from it; it becomes the ocean, and in becoming the ocean it knows the ocean. It is the same for human beings. They are finite and limited, but when they have worked a long time to purify themselves, they will awaken inner faculties and possibilities that are almost limitless – they will merge with the immensity, and they will know the eternal and infinite nature of God.

11 August

Simplicity can be defined as the constant effort to direct one's thoughts to the summit. For, it is at the summit that the spirit, the 1, reigns. When we are far from the summit, we do not have a clear view of things, we have no control over situations and everything becomes complicated. It is our lower nature that creates these complications. In its aim to satisfy its desires, it pushes people to scatter their energies and be superficial. They might find what they are seeking, for a short while, but by dispersing their energies in matter, in order to accumulate possessions and increase their pleasures, they limit themselves inwardly.

In Dante's *Divine Comedy*, he describes hell as an upside-down cone, and this image corresponds to reality. The more that humans behave in such a way as to distance themselves from the 1 – symbolically, the top of an upright cone – the more they are doomed to descend into the depths of the upside-down cone and suffer all its limitations. Only those who try to become simpler by climbing to the top will sense a growing inner potential to move, create and express themselves freely.

12 August

*H*ow many people there are who think they are capable of following a spiritual Master, when they are still full of thoughts, feelings and desires that prevent them from receiving what he says and putting it into practice! They have no space in them for such a teaching. And, often, it would be better if they kept themselves at a bit of a distance, because in wanting to walk a path that is not made for them they will one day find themselves in the grip of serious contradictions. They won't understand why nothing is happening the way they expected it to, and not only will they suffer but they will make others suffer too, and they will even hinder the work of the person they say they want to learn from.

Contrary to what some may believe, a spiritual Master is not fond of being surrounded by a crowd of people. He knows that his teaching is not for everyone. He simply hopes that, whatever level they are at, all those who come to him at least receive a few truths that will help them progress.

13 August

*T*he lords of karma decreed what every human's present life would be, based on how they lived their previous lives; these decrees are just. This is why, instead of complaining about the difficulties they encounter, people must tell themselves, 'If I am facing such and such a difficulty now, it is because, in a past incarnation, I didn't know how to, or didn't want to, solve the problems I was faced with then, and now they have come back again.'

Those people who rebel instead of understanding that their destiny is ruled by the laws of divine justice make their situation worse, and the problems they encounter will be more and more difficult to solve, and they will feel more and more restricted. Heaven's judges will say to them, 'So, you didn't want to learn your lesson even though you had the right conditions to do so? Well, now, here are the same problems. Try to start working with them; otherwise your situation will get even worse.' Instead of running away from difficulties, you should try to really understand their meaning and do what is needed to overcome them. That is how you become free.

14 August

*I*n every religion, there have always been – and still are – some members of the clergy who portray the Lord as a monarch or judge solely occupied with condemning the guilty. No, the truth is that God is always waiting in his palace for us to join his feasts. But in order to take part we must fulfil certain conditions.

Imagine a king invites you to a great meal: if you turn up dirty, with unkempt hair and in rags, the guards or sentries at the gate will tell you, 'It's not possible for you to come in.' 'But I've been invited!' 'We understand, but do you realize this is the royal palace? You can't go in looking like that.' It is not enough to be invited; you have to arrive suitably dressed, and those who turn up in a dirty and neglected inner state will not be received at the divine feast. They are not required to be dressed like royalty all the time, but for a while at least they must put on suitable clothes, meaning that they must make the effort to harmonize with the beings of light taking part in the feast.

15 August

*T*he only purpose of spiritual exercises is to enable human beings to merge with the divine. With each step they make toward achieving this, they become further detached from the false ideas they have of themselves and move closer to their true self. The new awareness they then develop becomes part of everything they do. They begin to feel like a different being, and little by little God himself becomes manifested in them. Initiates in India have summed up this work in the formula 'I am That', meaning: 'The divine alone exists, and I exist only inasmuch as I can become one with the divine.' And their disciples learn to meditate on this formula, which they repeat until it becomes their very flesh and bone.

It is very rare for human beings to succeed in raising themselves up to this peak, but by making efforts everyone can go beyond some of their limitations. Even those with a severe disability possess the means to go beyond themselves. If they are willing to turn their gaze and their thoughts to those inner regions where the divine spark shines, they will at least gain an intuition of their true predestination.

16 August

***H**uge advances in the sciences and in technology encourage our contemporaries to seek an easy life. But nowhere in nature do we find a programme for an easy life. Human beings are on earth to work, but to work above all on themselves, so that there will be constant inner progress. Of course, people go to work every day, but the main aim of all their activity is to provide material security for themselves and their family; it rarely nourishes their soul and spirit, which is why they wear themselves out.

It is spiritual work that strengthens, enlivens and rejuvenates. And when I say spiritual work, I am not necessarily thinking of meditation or prayer. Every activity we pursue, however modest, brings renewed energy, if we make the effort to accompany it with a feeling of love and with light-filled thoughts.

17 August

A true magus knows how to emit light. Not only is he surrounded and protected by his aura, it also provides him with the material for his work. It is thanks to this subtle matter that he is able to create and manifest his power. He doesn't even need to speak; he only has to send his thoughts out, and it is as if he were speaking. This inner speech, which is real, powerful and magical, is also called the Word.

The Word is a thought that has not yet been translated into words but already has expression in the invisible in the form of shapes, colours and sounds. Stones, plants, animals and humans all understand this language, and the planets, the stars, the angels and the archangels also understand it. In the invisible world, creatures speak to one another not by using words but by emanating colours, shapes and melodies, and each one immediately knows how to interpret this language.

18 August

*E*very day, while you are eating, you are helping to build, support and restore your body. And if, during the meal, you concentrate on the food so as to draw out the particles of divine life contained in it, you are working to renew the substance of your body. And not only eating but also breathing, washing and sleeping can all play a part in making your body a vessel, a temple, of God. You also need to watch your thoughts, your feelings and your wishes, for these too are forms of nourishment.

This temple of God that you have been building within you will remain invisible for a long time, for it is the result of long-term work. But, one day, the light emanating from your face and your whole being will show that the Lord has made his home in you. He will come to live in you with his angels, and the temple of your body will vibrate as one with the immense temple of nature.

19 August

***H**uman time is determined by the alternation of day and night. Different forms of day and night can be found everywhere, in all spheres. Take the seasons. What are spring and summer? They are day: the sun's influence becomes greater and greater. And what are autumn and winter? They are night: the moon, symbolically, takes back the power, as nature takes a rest to recuperate, in order for spring and summer to once again produce flowers and fruit.

A month can also be likened to a day: during the fourteen days when the moon is waxing, you could say it is day, and during the fourteen days when it is waning it is night. Sometimes, even in a single hour, you may have day under the sun's influence and night under the moon's, depending on the mood you are in. But, day or night, there is always mental work to do. Whatever the conditions, there is never any excuse for remaining inactive.

20 August

I*f* you place the idea of the Creator at the centre of your life, if you have faith in him, love him and base your hopes on him, you will be preparing the inner path along which you will continue to progress throughout your life. Each conviction you keep alive in you influences your destiny. On the psychic plane, as on the physical plane, the absence or presence of certain elements gives different results.

Ask a cook or chemist whether the presence or absence of certain ingredients in their cooking and their laboratory experiments gives the same results. The whole of life demonstrates the importance of an element being present or absent. So, it is even more important when it is a matter of the presence or absence in people's lives of the idea of God, of his wisdom and his love.

21 August

*M*ost people don't have a clear idea of what purity really is, and they tend to limit it mainly to the area of sexuality. For them sexual abstinence is purity.

In reality, something is pure when it has not been soiled and corrupted by selfish thoughts and passionate feelings of lust, jealousy and possessiveness. To be pure it is not enough to abstain from all sexual relations. If only it were that simple! Our thoughts, feelings and desires are the places where impurities find their way in. These impurities then produce consequences in people's general behaviour, including how they experience sexuality. But the sexual act can be experienced in the greatest purity.

22 *August*

*W*hy is the pentagram considered to be one of the most powerful magical figures? Because it offers analogies with our five fingers and, therefore, connects us to the five virtues linked to them: love, wisdom, truth, fairness and kindness.

Magi are traditionally depicted holding a wand, but really the wand is only an extension of their hand. Even if it is said to be magical, in itself it is nothing special, and anyone who got hold of even the greatest mage's wand shouldn't expect to perform extraordinary things with it. It is the hand of the person holding the wand that is powerful. Thanks to the work they have done on themselves – a work of purification, concentration and self-mastery – they have gained the power to harness energy currents from space and project them out using their hand. We still do not know everything the hand is capable of.

23 August

***H**appiness is a gift of the heart. To be happy, we have to expand our heart and keep on expanding it until it embraces the whole universe. It is love that opens the way to happiness. Yes, love, not science or philosophy. Those who are very knowledgeable do not necessarily find happiness, as we can see, whereas those who do not know very much but have a big heart feel happy.

The Creator has placed happiness in the heart, not in the mind. Science and wisdom can only prepare the path and give directions and explanations. To be happy we have to love, but with wisdom as our guide, so that we know which beings and which ventures to give our love to. Otherwise, we are asking to be greatly deceived, and we will be very unhappy. So, love and wisdom are connected. Wisdom shows love how to be more enlightened, and love shows wisdom how to become warmer.

24 August

*T*he sun and moon are not just in the sky – they are also present symbolically in our psychic life. The sun, the masculine principle, is represented in us by our spirit and our mind; the moon, the feminine principle, is represented by our soul and our heart.

When we are confronted by difficulties, it feels just as if we are battling against enemies, inner or outer ones. And it is best not to do that in the dark, meaning when the lower nature is expressing itself and perpetuating the upset and confusion. So that is the time to ask our inner sun and moon to keep shining in our sky. The sun – our mind enlightened by the spirit – will inspire us with the best thoughts. The moon – our heart enlightened by our soul – will inspire us with the best feelings. And their light will be with us until we win the battle.

25 August

*T*he dangers that lie in wait for the followers of a spiritual teaching are weakness and vulnerability. Too often, because they have chosen the path of light, they tend to imagine that, as they progress, they will be protected by powerful entities and be safe from setbacks, illnesses and attacks from people wishing them harm. This makes them vulnerable, and when they have to confront difficulties they were not expecting, they do not know how to face them and collapse.

From now on, every one of you must be aware that a spiritual teaching does not prepare a refuge for you where you will be safe from life's trials, but, in giving you light and methods, it does so much more! Whatever life brings, allow this light in, practise these methods, and you will remain solid and unshakeable in the midst of difficulties. God's grace does not fall on human beings randomly: it falls only on those who never leave the path of light and who have begun the real work.

26 August

***H**umans spend much of their time destroying themselves through the way they live and the thoughts, feelings and desires they have. So, they do not love themselves, or rather they don't love themselves very well. You will ask, 'So, what do we have to do to love ourselves well?' Learn to love the Lord first, because in loving God you already love yourself, but it is your higher self, your true self, the self that is a fragment of the Divine.

When we love God, it does not mean we love a being outside of us, but a being that lives within us, which is our sublime self. If we do not love this self, if we do not love God within us, what we love is our lower self. That is what we serve and devote our time and energies to. Then all we do is impoverish ourselves and become weaker, because the lower self is an abyss that swallows up all our energies. A true love of self must pass by way of a love for God. In loving God we love ourselves – our divine part. Thanks to this love we raise ourselves up to the world of beauty, light and freedom.

27 August

*A*strologers seek to determine the influences that planets exert on humans. Actually, for each one of us, the nature of these influences depends on the quality of our aura. For, one of the aura's functions is to provide exchanges between the stars in the sky and our inner stars.

I think you are surprised, aren't you, to hear that the planets exist in us too? Since humans are a reflection of the cosmos, the planets also exist in us, and, just as they do in the universe, they revolve around our inner sun. If the same planet affects some people favourably and others unfavourably, it is simply because the ones who receive its bad influences are not ready to pick up its good ones. If there are elements in their aura that prevent a planet's good qualities from entering them, the currents this planet sends become distorted, break up and produce harmful effects. If, on the other hand, their aura is pure and powerful, all influences, even those that could be harmful, become good.

28 August

The spirit works constantly on matter by fertilizing it, and as new creations appear it discovers its powers and comes to know itself. So, when some people ask why God created the world, we can reply, 'To know himself'. He created suns, planets, stones, plants, animals and humans in order to know himself.

In the same way, human beings, having been created in God's image, need to work with matter to learn who they are. Their spirit is immersed in matter – the matter of their physical body, which is a microcosm of the universe – and they seek to know themselves through it. And when will they truly know themselves? When they have worked to make this matter, which now envelops and imprisons them, become so subtle and transparent that it reflects their true image. Until then, human beings cannot know themselves – it's as if they are at a distance from themselves, lost in the opaqueness of matter.

29 August

*V*isible fire is the expression of the invisible fire. This is why, each time you light a fire, even a simple candle, you can link to the heavenly fire through your soul and spirit. Contemplate this fire until it sets your heart, your soul and your entire being alight. You may read or hear every explanation about the descent of the Spirit into human beings, but it will be of no use to you so long as you are not trying to light a fire in your soul – the fire that will make you a living being, alive like the sun, for the sun is the visible, sentient form of the spiritual fire.

And since the sun rises each morning, each morning you can reconnect through it with the heavenly fire and allow it to set you alight, until the day when you feel flames bursting from the depths of your being. It is the sun that reveals the mystery of fire to us. By linking ourselves to it with all our love and all our intelligence, we will continue to walk tirelessly towards it. To reach this fire, we have to follow the path of initiation.

30 August

*J*ust as children want to be at least the equal of their father or mother, so disciples take their Master as their role model. But the ideal they should be aiming for is not their father, their mother or their Master but God himself, who created them in his own image. The Master is a gateway, a staging point, a teacher for a while. Nowhere is it written that disciples must go no further than him. Through their Master, they must go to God. And if their Master has reached God, they will be with him close to God.

'The one who believes in me will also do the works that I do and, in fact, will do greater works than these', said Jesus in the gospels. Jesus wanted his followers to do great things, even greater than he had done. Is that possible? Yes, and if Jesus spoke in such an impersonal and selfless way, it is because he was not working for his own glory but was doing God's work, to bring about his kingdom on earth.

31 August

*Y*our daily life is made up of exchanges with the outer world, but you should be more concerned with your inner world, because you have to deal with that all the time. You are not always watching, listening, touching or tasting something outside of you, but you are always with yourself, with your thoughts, your feelings and your desires – these never stop. It is just a question of knowing what you must do with them.

As long as the outside world is the main focus of your attention and your expectations, you will be disappointed. Maybe, for a time, you will be able to imagine you have hold of something, but after a while you will be forced to admit that you have nothing anymore – everything has left you. Are you looking for happiness, for love, for meaning in your life? You must look for them first and foremost in yourself.

1 September

*M*ost traditions associate the right-hand side with good, and the left-hand side with evil. When it is said of someone that they follow the left-hand path, it means their behaviour is not great. But in daily life, our left hand must unite with our right hand so we may act efficiently.

Our left hand and our right hand are both instruments for our activity. They work together in unison, in harmony and complement each other; each one is an aspect of the unity we represent. We cannot see one hand independently from the other, for they are polarised: our right hand is emissive and has the masculine polarity, and our left hand is receptive and has the feminine polarity. This is why they have often been related to the sun (our right hand) and the moon (our left hand), which both influence us. The masculine principle and the feminine principle project currents through both our hands and they act together to work, support, repair and save.

2 *September*

Receiving a new philosophy that opens new horizons and presents an increasingly high ideal to attain, supposes you are able to harmonise yourselves with it and therefore reinforce not only your brain, but also your stomach, lungs and your whole body, to be able to withstand the tensions that will necessarily arise. You must not imagine that the currents of light and love are easy to bear. Spirituality is first of all a science you acquire by listening to a sage talk and by reading different works. But just feeding your intellect is not sufficient, and may even be detrimental.

Those who decide to follow a spiritual teaching must also change their way of life. If not, after some time, they will fall prey to contradictions such that they will be in conflict not only with themselves, but also with society and those around them. Many people, after embracing spiritual life, have become intolerable for those around them. They would do best to do some soul-searching: they will see if they create harmony around them and if they are deserving of the spiritual teaching they have decided to follow.

3 September

Would you like to be more alive? Would you like your vibrations and emanations to intensify? Among the dozens of methods I can give you, retain at least one of them. Become aware of all the life present around you, everywhere in nature, but also in human beings. When greeting the people you meet, try to sense the spark of divine life in them, thank them for everything they give you or do for you, sometimes even without your knowing it. Being alive is about always being filled with wonder, always seeing people and things around us and above us as if it were for the first time.

Life is the strongest link connecting us to God, and even if it is possible to find religion in churches, it is above all present in nature. This is why we must maintain a conscious connection with all its most powerful and beautiful manifestations. We continue this study of life over millions of years, for it is an endless science, and this is what makes it so captivating. Once we have begun, we sense we will never be able to stop.

4 September

Due to the earth's rotation, the sun does not rise at the same time everywhere in the world. But that does not matter much; whether it is daytime or night-time where you are, somewhere on the earth the sun is rising on the horizon. So even during the night, through thought you can go to where the sun is rising: you therefore join those who are busy contemplating it and participate in their meditation and their prayers. And if one morning you wake up a little too late to see the sun rise where you are, it's a shame of course, but nothing stops you from going by thought towards the west where you will find the sun: in this way, you will not have lost all of dawn's blessings.

And don't think human beings are the only ones who watch the sun rise. There are billions of spirits in the invisible who turn to the sun and nourish themselves with its warmth and light. Humans are the last ones to know how to receive the sun's energies. Plants surpass them in this regard.

5 September

Sometimes you might unexpectedly receive a light, a blessing from heaven. Be conscious of it and stop for a long moment to let it permeate you.

Most human beings don't realize that most of their suffering comes from the fact that they lack this awareness. How often do they receive an inspiration, an impulse and support from the spiritual world, but they very soon lose them simply through their neglect and lack of consideration for the value of what they received. They act as if heaven will always be there to serve them, and when they have nothing more interesting to do, they accept to stop for a few moments to listen to what it has to tell them and receive what it has to give them. Well no, heaven is not at the disposal of superficial and careless people! If they are not attentive enough to sense what heaven gives their soul and spirit, they will be given nothing more.

6 September

*A*ny confusion or malaise we might feel warns us that an 'enemy' is after us. To escape, we must seek to reach our higher consciousness and lock ourselves away there, like in a fortress, and not leave, not even to ward off the enemy threatening us.

How often have people who tried to fight off their enemies, like certain tendencies and bad instincts, had to admit that all they did was make them even stronger! So forget about these enemies and only concentrate on going within to find refuge in your higher self. On these heights you rise up to, you will receive light, wisdom and strength, and you will then be able to defend yourselves with true weapons.

7 September

*A*ll materialist philosophies around the world create deplorable teaching methods. The catastrophic effects are more and more visible in adolescents who are inwardly deprived of light and of a solid support base.

Whatever some people may think, educating children without making them aware of the Creator's presence, of the reality of the world of the soul and the spirit, and of the need to maintain a connection with it, does not give the same results as when they are deprived of these notions. Life's events unfold in a completely different way for them. Or rather, they have the same difficulties and obstacles as anyone else, but they have other means, forces and powers which the others are denied, having not learnt from a very young age to weave ties with the divine world. And so, in situations where others weaken and become discouraged or take tortuous paths, they instead progress and better themselves, and support and enlighten those around them.

8 September

T*rue clairvoyance, our true eyes are found in our heart; for it is love that opens our eyes. When you love someone, you see all sorts of beautiful things in them that no one else sees. Those who don't have this love for them may think you exaggerate, but you see this person just as God originally created them, or just like they will be when they return to the bosom of the Eternal.

Only love has the power to open our spiritual eyes. People who wish to become clairvoyant must learn to love. For if they don't love, they are blind to other people's magnificent qualities and to the wonders of nature. And not only do they not see them, they also constantly criticize the Creator for having done things so badly: in his place, they would have done things differently... and better, of course! But so long as their heart is closed, they will be unable to enter the kingdom of mysteries.

9 September

'Our Father, who are in heaven' is how Jesus teaches us to pray in the Gospel, and we ask this Father, *'Give us today our daily bread'*, that is to say the quantity of food we need to get through the day. There is no need to ask for any more than that. The amount we need for the present day must suffice.

This bread – the symbol of the food required for our physical life – must also and above all be understood on the spiritual plane. Each morning, we must seek this heavenly bread, and we don't need to stock up with it for several days. The next day, we will ask for it again. Every day, we must seek this food that is forever new – light, wisdom and love – and that we find in the rising sun's life, light and warmth. But understand me well: I am not only talking about the physical sun here, I am also, and especially, talking about the spiritual sun.

10 September

Culture and civilisation are nothing more than work on matter. Human beings will always have work to do with it and on it, but this work of creation is not to be limited to the physical matter outside of them. Their instincts, desires, feelings and thoughts are also matter they must aim to work on to purify and ennoble it.

Spiritual work is therefore also work on matter. When humans learn to use all the powers of the spirit to work on the matter within them, everything they will then realize on the outside will be marked with the seal of the spirit, with its light, its love and its power.

11 September

When a gesture, a word or a look makes you tense or angry, you may of course retaliate. But if you wish to act wisely, don't move, and above all, keep quiet! Anger is like an eruption of the brute force of a torrent; this force is not necessarily a bad thing and it can even be beneficial to you and to others, but provided you know how to control it so as to then be able to guide it. And to control it, you must first lay down the weapons this instinctive reaction suddenly gave you. So at first, don't move and don't respond.

And then, to overcome the tension you may still be feeling, take a deep breath, make some harmonious and rhythmical movements with your legs, arms and head. You might also want to, in thought, write some words in the space around you with letters of light, such as peace, wisdom, love, beauty and so on. These very simple methods give great results, provided you keep enough lucidity and control to have the reflexes to use them.

12 September

We have seen people who were willing to sacrifice the entire world to save their family. They may have been able to ensure their safety and material well-being, but is this protection enough? Shelter and material comfort have never stopped anyone from suffering when they lack the essential: spiritual nourishment. It is only possible to give them this spiritual nourishment if we ourselves seek to progress each day on the path of the light.

There is no doubt that most human beings love their family, but they don't yet know how to truly do them good. Nor do they know that thanks to the tie linking them to their loved ones, they can have a positive influence on them even when they have left the earth, for these parents' souls will always be there, near them, and take part in their life. If their sons and daughters study and improve themselves, these parents in the other world will also benefit from the efforts they make. And when these sons and daughters themselves have children, their children will inherit the spiritual riches they acquired.

13 September

*T*o understand why the number 13 is considered to be evil, we must first consider the number 12 for a moment. A day is made up of two times twelve hours, a year of twelve months and there are twelve signs of the zodiac, and so on. 12 is therefore the number that forms a whole, a complete set. But 13 is 12 + 1. The 1 that is added does not belong to the set formed by the number 12; it is considered a foreign element, and if it is not pure and disinterested, if it does not vibrate in unison with the whole to which it is added, the whole set itself is threatened. This is why the number 13 is seen as a difficult number that brings hardship and even death: the thirteenth card in the Tarot deck is that of death.

Now, we could also say that the 1 added to the 12 represents the beginning of another cycle or of another set. In Initiatic Science, death is never seen as an ending or an end beyond which there is nothing more, but instead as the beginning of a new life.

14 September

*D*isciples of Initiatic Science, through their thoughts, feelings and ideals, seek to bring about transformation to even the very heart of their own cells. They know that the billions of cells making up their physical body are home to small souls and that each one of them was given a specific activity. For a cell is not a simple particle of matter occupying any old place in the body. Each cell behaves like a worker who knows the work they must carry out in the part of the body where they are situated, and the smooth functioning of the whole depends on the work they do.

It is hard to explain the connection linking human beings to all the souls in their body. But this connection does exist and it becomes very strong when a person realizes that, through the life they lead and through a work of thought, they can link with their cells and regenerate them. In seeking to master, purify and enrich their own psychic life, not only do they influence the physical particles in their body, but they also have an effect on their memory; and so all their bad tendencies and bad habits gradually give way to new and better behaviour.

15 September

*E*very house and building is covered by a roof. According to the eternal language of symbols, a roof symbolizes the world of the spirit, and everyone must seek the inspiration of the spirit to avoid giving in to disorder and confusion. When disorder breaks out around you or within you, try to climb onto your roof and remain there; that is to say, try to think and analyze, and connect with the divine world so you may find peace and light. Only then will you be able to see clearly and know the decisions to make.

Whatever the physical or psychic dangers we may be exposed to, by climbing onto the roof, by projecting ourselves into the spiritual world, we have the best chance of finding the solutions for acting efficiently in matter. For matter never totally guarantees us salvation. Good material conditions are useful, but even the most favourable ones do not keep us safe forever. And it goes even further than that, because if we don't turn to the spirit to know how to put favourable material circumstances to the best use, they can turn against us.

16 September

*E*ach of us comes into the world endowed with a particular psychic make-up, and because of this we are inclined to take on certain opinions and tastes rather than others, and to adopt certain behaviour. This is natural and normal. But we also come into the world with critical faculties, with powers of reason that help us to make choices in all of this. So instead of being carried away by our impulses, we must at the very least say to ourselves, 'Alright, I see and feel things in a certain way, but some people are perhaps better informed than I am, because they have studied much longer. For the time being, I am not going to express myself until I too have studied.'

How often do we hear people saying, 'As for me, I think …Personally, I find that…' with the conviction that they are in the right. But even if their points of view are justified, there is always progress to be made. Yes, everyone's intelligence and conduct can always be improved.

17 September

*T*rue love is not a feeling but a state of consciousness. Those who cultivate true love as a state of consciousness see everything anew, for love has this extraordinary capacity of making us see human beings, nature and the creatures inhabiting it as we were seeing them for the first time.

Only love is able to sense the subtle currents of life that pass through us, and these currents are constantly being renewed. Objective and physical knowledge of what exists is not enough to fulfil us. Take for example someone who might be capable of exploring the entire universe: they would end up feeling a void, and even feeling bored if they have not learnt to make contact with the subtle currents of life that flow through all beings and through everything.

18 September

Whatever your degree of evolution, always try to further explore your consciousness and develop your faculties even more.

Here is an exercise. First of all, remain silent and still for a while, and then through thought, rise up. Imagine you are gradually leaving your body through the opening at the top of your skull. Keep imagining yourself rising through your causal, buddhic and atmic bodies, linking to the universal Soul, the cosmic Principle that fills all of space and, there, you participate in its work in all regions of the universe at the same time. Although you may not know clearly what you are doing, your spirit will know.

19 September

*P*eople who are interested in Initiatic Science must study the beyond, starting with the relationship between human beings and the universe. Humans are made up of various regions, just like the universe: their physical, astral, mental, causal, buddhic and atmic bodies, through which they are connected to all the regions in space. According to the nature of their thoughts, feelings, desires and actions, they contact the world of light or the world of darkness. When humans die, they only leave their physical body. If during their life they tried to dominate the manifestations of their lower nature, and they purified their astral and mental bodies, thanks to the law of affinity, they will head for the higher astral and mental planes of beauty and joy, and if not, they will be drawn to the lower astral and mental planes where they will suffer.

Before being regions in space where humans go after they die to either suffer or to rejoice, what Christians called hell and paradise are above all regions present within humans – these regions are part of them and they cannot escape them.

20 September

What do faith, hope and love mean for most human beings? Some people might remember as children having heard in church about these three 'theological' virtues, meaning they relate to God. But all that is now far away and may not mean much to them anymore. And yet, all human beings, whoever they may be, love and have hope and faith.

If these three virtues seem distant and foreign to them it is because they see them as something abstract. They don't consider them as pillars of their inner life because they don't yet see God as a living reality and they don't really know how to imagine him. How often have I told you that the best image of God is given to us by the sun, the giver of life, light and warmth. Only the sun's life, light and warmth can make us feel the power, wisdom and love of God. It is therefore up to us to connect with this divine power, wisdom and love, and we can only do so with hope, faith and love.

21 September

*W*e must know how to discern our higher self from our lower self so as to encourage the expressions of our higher self only. We must also have the same attitude when it comes to others, and always seek to contact their divine nature to give it the possibility to reveal itself and flourish.

So often, humans constantly feed the lower nature of members of their family, of their friends and those around them on the pretext of responding to their wishes and needs! They don't know that humans' lower nature is characterized by greed, self-centredness and ingratitude; and while they think they can attract love and recognition from them, in reality they set themselves up for the worst disappointments. In return for their services, all they receive is indifference, contempt and sometimes even hatred. And then they complain and say, 'After all I have done for him - or for her!' Well, instead of sacrificing themselves for others, they should have asked themselves what they were serving in them: their higher nature or their lower nature.

22 *September*

We shouldn't be surprised that so many people nowadays claim they no longer believe in God or deny he exists. They can no longer accept the puerile and simplistic image they are given of God; and since they have no idea what to replace it with, they ask themselves useless questions about his existence. But they won't get any answers by wondering about the presence of God. We obtain answers by working to deepen our awareness of a life and a presence. We can only discover the reality of God within ourselves.

Human beings have now made great progress in their knowledge of the psychic world. It is therefore possible for them to understand that this God that they still see as a being exterior to themselves is in reality within them. Only then will they acquire true riches and power. Those who see God outside themselves are left to their own limited resources. While those who realize they are inseparable from the Creator, not only do they lack nothing, but they also see more and more clearly so as to face their difficulties and do good around them.

23 September

Someone who has achieved great spiritual elevation can make themselves heard by spiritual entities and attract them thanks to the power of their aura without raising their voice and without making gestures with their hands. Their speech is only an aid, and any effect it produces is because it is permeated with this creative element, with the Word and the light.

To a lesser degree of course, each one of you can experiment the power of the Word. On some days, when you speak, you may have no effect on the people you speak to. But at other times, on the contrary, you will impress them with the very same words: your speech is alive and so they listen to you. It is alive because the words you say are imbued with the subtle matter of your aura; thanks to it they are stronger and this power enables them to reach people's soul and make it vibrate. The same is true with the look in your eyes – it is also like words: it is infused with the light matter of your aura and it has a beneficial effect on others.

24 September

We all have an entire population within us – our cells – and we are responsible for them. We can protect them, but only if we give them pure air to breathe and healthy food and drink. If not, after trying to resist, they will become weak and will no longer be able to withstand the attacks from the outside: all the forms of pollution and epidemics that threaten them. In order to provide them with food and clean air, we must also do work on our thoughts and feelings because our cells too are sensitive to the psychic atmosphere we create.

This is true science, the science of life. You might say it is a strange science. Maybe, but when we will one day have instruments capable of studying humans' inner life, we will discover that nothing is more precise than the science of our inner life, the science of thought and feeling, and of their effects on our psychic and physical health.

25 September

*F*rom the summit where they are perched, proud people always look downward, and obviously, all they can see are those who are ignorant, weak and wicked. They view them with contempt and go about swollen with a feeling of superiority. But since they are always self-satisfied, they don't progress.

While those who look upward notice others who are wiser, more evolved and filled with light, and so in comparison, they begin to notice their own faults. They feel very small compared to others – they become humble and this humility makes them grow. By focussing their attention on other people and admiring them, they don't remain idle: they work and make an effort – they wish to become like the others! This is how they progress.

26 September

***H**uman beings' hands constitute one of their main instruments of creation, not only on the physical plane, but also on the psychic and spiritual planes. For hands are not restricted to their physical contours only – they extend into the subtle planes where they not only pick up currents and forces, but also project them.

You use your hands everyday and you know how limited you would be if you were to lose the use of them. But you are not sufficiently aware that your hands are not just physical organs like any tool or instrument; the fluidic matter that emanates from you links them to the subtle body of nature. The hands of those who have worked with love and wisdom over much time truly enter in communication with the heavenly powers and transmit their blessings.

27 September

*P*eople see and hear so many things that most of them end up becoming swamped and indifferent. They allow their attention to skim over things without resting anywhere, and nothing makes an impression on them any more: they look without seeing and listen without hearing. Habit rules their life and nothing can be more pernicious than letting themselves be ruled by habit – it deadens them.

Actually, the only habit to adopt is that of not becoming accustomed to anything, and of always looking at ideas, beings or objects in a new way, with a fresh eye. Observe them, study them as if you were meeting them for the first time – you will then discover connections between them, and something of the life of the universe will reveal itself to you. From time to time, also try to breathe and eat as if for the first time.

28 September

*T*hrough his words, a spiritual Master strives to lead his disciples as far as he can; then he must be silent. It is impossible for him to reveal everything he experiences in his spirit and soul. A Master can only try to assure his disciples that experiences that are still unimaginable to them are in fact real. And because these experiences permeate his whole being, they also permeate everything he tells them. Whatever the subject matter, what he passes on to his disciples comes from a very high and distant place. In this way he gives them the desire to experience what he himself has experienced, and through his explanations and the methods he gives, he prepares the conditions for them and shows them the way.

Never forget that I only tell you about your life and the realities and possibilities you have within you. Even if you are not already aware of them, even if you don't quite understand what I am telling you, I know that through what I say, I connect with an entity in you, one that is waiting to come to light.

29 September

*T*o be able to work on humanity, a spiritual Master needs a collective body. In this collective body, some of his disciples represent the eyes, the ears or the mouth; while others represent the brain, the heart and so on. For as long as he cannot bring this collective body to life, the Master is weak and his spirit has difficulty expressing the full extent of his wisdom, love and power.

A Master's spirit first had to make an effort to incarnate in his own physical body, but it also has to incarnate in the collective body of a spiritual community in order for this community to continue to grow in the light. And of course, this spiritual body must also make an effort to help their Master's spirit manifest in it. This is why, instead of remaining focussed on the image of their Master and repeating how much they admire him, how much they love him and are privileged to have such a Master, each disciple should only be preoccupied with helping him. How? By seeking to become a pure and luminous particle in the collective body their Master is trying to bring to life in order to continue his powerful work in the world.

30 September

Contrary to what is too commonly thought, putting yourselves in the service of God does not imply you must neglect your fellow humans, on the contrary. True sons and daughters of God are those who seek to serve him in their fellow humans too. And even if they only receive ungratefulness in return, they don't become discouraged. They have settled and overcome their personal, financial and social problems and are free to think further and higher. They feel they are members of the universal family and in working for it, their soul finds its food.

It is true that not everyone is ready for this work. Those who dedicate themselves to the good of all people must not expect to lead a peaceful life, for they will even have to face more difficulties than anyone else. But since they are a servant of God, the beings of light that also serve the Lord come to their rescue and carry part of their load. They are not supported on the physical and material planes, but on the psychic and spiritual planes. It is there they receive the light and the strength to better withstand adversity and to continue their work.

1 October

*E*very month, we see the moon waxing and waning in the sky. Similarly, our consciousness brightens and dims, ebbs and flows. We are subject to the same alternations as nature, and it is therefore necessary to be aware of the time when each phenomenon is likely to occur. Imagine a difficult period is nearing – if you don't feel it coming, you unwisely take on commitments; then, when it is time to act, you no longer have the inspiration or the desire and you fail in your endeavour. You could have avoided this failure had you anticipated there would inevitably come a time when you would see less clearly. For all errors are made in the dark, at the moment when our consciousness is clouded.

You cannot escape this alternation of day and night, light and darkness within you anymore than you can outside. But if you learn to observe yourself, each time you will discover certain warning signs alerting you to the approaching period of darkness. So be vigilant. Prepare the spiritual elements that will continue to maintain the light within you.

2 October

On the physical plane, the four elements have the ability to either mutually reinforce or neutralize each another. Air fans fire or blows it out. Water also extinguishes fire, but fire can turn it into steam. Earth, for its part, absorbs water.

We can find equivalent phenomena on the psychic plane. I have given you exercises to do with earth, because on the psychic plane, earth also has the power to absorb bad currents which are comparable to water. When you feel troubled or irritated, make a small hole in the ground, place a finger in it and ask the entities that work in its bowels to absorb these negative states. These days, the changes occurring in society are such that humans have less and less contact with the earth; this is a shame, because this contact is always beneficial to the psyche. On several occasions, I have advised people who were suffering from anxiety or obsession to work the land. Ploughing, digging, weeding and planting can be done as therapy.

3 October

What is a talisman and what is a pentacle? A talisman is an object (a stone, flower, insect, ring, bracelet, and so on) that nature itself, or a psychically powerful being has infused with energy. A pentacle is a figure that has been engraved in metal or stone, painted on parchment, or even embroidered on a piece of cloth, and on which letters are also inscribed. Many pentacles bear words written in Hebrew for according to Cabbalah, each letter of the Hebrew alphabet relates to a geometric form that exists in nature, and specific forces act through each geometric form.

Therefore, someone who knows how each letter relates to invisible powers can trigger cosmic currents: by writing or engraving certain forms, they establish communication with the corresponding entities in the hereafter. When an initiate seeks to understand the relationships between forces, forms and letters, and the way in which to use them, they do so in order to establish a beneficial link between the earth and heaven, between the world below and the world above.

4 October

*M*any researchers acknowledge having found the solution to the problems preoccupying them in their sleep. Indeed, during sleep, the soul travels and comes into contact with other worlds. When we hear about scientific research, we tend to imagine people in laboratories, busy working on devices and filling entire pages with calculations. It is true that they handle devices and do a lot of calculations, but if we studied their case closely, we would learn that their unconscious often plays a big role in their discoveries.

The perseverance and intensity of the efforts made by some researchers sometimes puts them in an almost out-of-body state; they are propelled into unknown regions they never even imagined, which is why the moment when they least expect it, the solution comes to them like a flash of lightning. And this can occur while they are sleeping – they suddenly awaken, quickly note something down, then fall back to sleep; the next day, they barely remember what happened. And if you know how to prepare yourself for sleep, you too may also receive certain revelations.

5 October

Only fusion, union and ecstasy allow humans to know God. The hexagram can be used as a symbol to clarify the process by which a human being melts into the Divine.

This geometrical figure, which spiritual science calls Solomon's Seal, is made of two intertwined equilateral triangles: one pointing upwards and the other pointing downwards. These two triangles represent the two universal processes of evolution and involution: the evolution of matter reaching towards the spirit (the triangle pointing upwards) and the involution of the spirit descending towards matter to vivify it (the triangle pointing down). These two figures teach us how we can elevate ourselves up to the Divine to melt into it, and as we rise, an inverse movement occurs – the Divine descends to live and manifest itself in us.

6 October

*T*hose who work for the good of the collective whole become workers in the field of the Lord. The spirits of light draw close to them to mark them with their seal. And once they have been marked, it is as if they were listed in a registry: what they are owed is recorded next to their name, and every day they receive a letter, or one might also say a ‘salary’. This salary comes in various forms: strength for the spirit, expansion for the soul, light for the intellect, warmth for the heart, health for the physical body.

We can use another image and say that these beings are connected to a kind of power station: currents descend through the subtle wires that connect them to this station and penetrate them, setting their psychic and spiritual devices in motion. In a house, all sorts of appliances begin to work as soon as we plug them into electrical sockets. It is the same with a human being. Just how many transmitters and receptors does each human possess in their different bodies! If they keep them in good working order, when the celestial current passes through them, a whole new life will awaken inside of them and begin to circulate.

7 October

Earth is a school, a learning centre to which we descend for many reasons, and mainly to settle the debts we incurred in our previous incarnations due to our mistakes. We must also understand the conditions that have been given to us in this life, and finally, seek to perfect ourselves in all areas.

Most humans, not knowing why they are on earth, content themselves with ensuring their well-being and satisfying their desires. Whereas someone who is enlightened knows they are here to fix the mistakes made in their past lives. They also try to understand why they incarnated in a such and such a country, such and such a family, and what this situation requires of them. Finally, they strive to develop all the seeds of the qualities and virtues the Creator has placed within them since eternity. This is why an initiatic school is so essential: nothing surpasses the light it brings to a disciple about the meaning of their earthly life.

8 October

Spiritual exercises like prayer and meditation are a form of communion. But not everyone necessarily has the time, the conditions, or even the inclination and gifts for spiritual practice. However, each of us is obliged to eat every day. It is therefore possible to start by learning to commune during meals, by showing more consideration for our food.

What is communing? To make a trade – you receive one thing and you give another. If you do not give anything, it is not true communion. True communion is a divine exchange. If in exchange for what the food gives you, you give it your attention and love, it will transform itself not only into physical energy within you, but also into psychic and spiritual energy, because you enter into relation with nature itself – the body of God. If, as you are about to start eating, you are conscious that God has put his life into the food, through you, the cells in your body will receive true communion: a spiritual element to help them in their work for the good of your whole body.

9 October

Everyone knows how important it is to pay attention, but attention has many facets. The best-known facet is the sustained application that is required to do our work properly, to understand what we are told, to study, and so on. But there is also another form of attention called self-observation. It entails becoming aware of what is happening inside of us at every moment of the day, of discerning the currents, the desires, the thoughts that pass through us, the influences, and the tension that we feel. It is this attention that is not sufficiently developed.

If you happen to be visited by thoughts and feelings that rob you of your courage, your confidence or your joy, it is because you are not attentive, not vigilant. And it is this appetite for easiness and for pleasures that dulls your vigilance. Indeed, how can one be vigilant when one only wants to indulge in what is easy and pleasant? It is like a dampness that settles on the wings of the soul and prevents it from flying. And when your soul can no longer fly, any dark entity from the invisible world can seize hold of it and take away your peace, your joy and your hope.

10 October

At the time when oil lamps were used for lighting, the glass tube had to be cleaned often to remove the build-up of smoke. Otherwise, even if the wick was lit, the lamp would not provide enough light. Fortunately, we now have electricity.

Why am I talking to you about oil lamps? Because human beings are like lamps. If they feed their flame with oil, that is to say if they give in to coarse, vulgar feelings, these are deposited as smoke or soot in their astral body, and the light inside them – the rays of their higher self – cannot cut through this opaque layer. They therefore remain in darkness, blind to the divine world, until the day they learn to burn better fuels: feelings that emit no impurities. If initiates and the wise see things that others cannot see, it is because they have worked long and hard to make their psychic matter transparent: a whole subtle world is made visible to them by their higher self whose rays are far-reaching.

11 October

*T*o live a spiritual life, one's spirit must be free. However, it is difficult for people to have a free spirit when they have an entire fortune to maintain, and even to amass – not to mention the temptations it presents. Why give up all their pleasures when they have so many means of satisfying their desires?

But leading a spiritual life is not simply a question of abandoning one's possessions. There is no point in renouncing material wealth unless we also rid ourselves of the thoughts, feelings and desires that cloud our inner sight. Those who do not know what true spirituality is may imagine that by giving up their material goods, they will find salvation. So, they flee society to seek refuge in monasteries or elsewhere, only to find emptiness. And even worse – deprived of all the activities and distractions the outside world has to offer, instead of meeting presences of light, they are confronted with their own demons. Before forgoing material goods, we must ensure that we possess enough inner riches to be able to live the life of the soul and the spirit.

12 October

When you plant a seed in the ground, it immediately establishes ties, since many of the elements in the soil will nurture it. But it also establishes contact with the sky: the rain waters it, the sun sends it its light and heat, and it begins to sprout. By simply planting a seed or a pit, you call upon the earth and sky to participate in its growth.

Similar processes occur within us too. For example, when we put a seed (food) into our earth (our stomach), our sky (our brain) immediately sends currents to our stomach, setting it to work to transform this food into energy. As a result, our whole body benefits, including our brain itself. When we connect the earth and sky, down below with up above, exchanges occur thanks to these connections. But when we break the connections, these exchanges are disrupted. To tie and untie – we find these two operations in all areas of life.

13 October

*I*n our physical body, each of our organs' cells has a memory-bearing etheric double. All of our cells, especially those making up the grey matter and white matter of our brain and solar plexus, record our actions, desires, feelings and thoughts. These recordings are kinds of negatives or prints, and once etched, they tend to repeat themselves – this is how habits come to be. So, if you want to replace old habits with new and better ones, you must change these imprints by striving to act according to the new orientation you wish to acquire. This requires constant vigilance, but tell yourself that vigilance is the secret to success.

So make sure that every gesture, every word, every thought, every feeling becomes an opportunity to etch the prints of a new life within you. These new negatives put you in contact with the regions of light in the universe. And because these regions dwell within you too, they will give you the purest currents and the most precious particles to create within you the body that initiatic tradition calls the body of glory.

14 October

*S*o many abominations have been committed in the name of God's love that more and more people are abandoning this distant Divinity who was a pretext for waging 'holy' wars, and they are now insisting on respect for the human person. That is all well and good. But in reality, those who have no consideration for some superior presence within each and every being cannot truly respect humans, for their lower nature will prevent them from doing so. They will only be able to respect their fellow humans once they have respect for something much greater than 'the human person'.

Humans must not place too much faith in what comes from their mind and heart, for though they certainly contain good things, they also contain greed, violence and possessiveness. That is why, even if they care for the well-being of others, if they are to maintain the right course, they must never forget the Creator. Otherwise, their thoughts and feelings will be so unenlightened that they will make others suffer and also hurt themselves.

15 October

Whatever your age, strive to be confident children, rejoicing in the smallest things, quickly forgetting vexations and failures – children with a heart always ready to love. This way you will never grow old.

If Cosmic Intelligence makes humans inevitably pass from childhood to old age, it is because old age also brings very good things. Symbolically, we can say that childhood and old age correspond to the two main virtues we have to develop. The child represents love wanting to act and manifest all the possibilities of life; the old person represents wisdom, analyzing and drawing conclusions from all their experiences. The child and the old person – love and wisdom – must learn to walk hand in hand: with love in the heart and with wisdom in the intellect. The heart must remain eternally young, and the intellect must become very old.

16 October

*T*he relationship between the spirit and the body has, from the very beginning, been one of the questions that human beings have struggled to solve. So many so-called spiritualists consider the body to be 'the tomb of the spirit'. They must learn to reason better. If the body were such a prison, if it were so opposed to human evolution, why would Cosmic Intelligence have sent them to incarnate on earth? They should remain pure spirits on high. Yet, in those who neglect their physical body on the pretext of devoting themselves to the noble functions of the intellect, the soul and the spirit, these very functions end up weakening and declining.

In reality, the manifestation of the spirit in humans is prevented not so much by their physical body, but rather by the fluidic shell made up of the desires, lusts and conflicts of their lower nature. If it were not continually generating all sorts of miasmas and fumes, their body would become a perfect instrument for the spirit.

17 October

***B**elievers of all religions have it as their first article of faith that God is the Creator of heaven and earth. They recite it in their prayers and sing it in their hymns, but then return to their usual occupations. Up above, the sun, the moon and the stars rise and set; on earth, flowers bloom, fruits ripen, streams flow, and so on. All of nature endlessly glorifies the Creator by celebrating his work.

And meanwhile what do humans do? They get together to glorify certain individuals who exhibit some talents, qualities or virtues, or to glorify themselves. Giving glory to God is not one of their concerns. Even those who have glorified him for a moment during their prayers or their hymns then think more about addressing their grievances and pleas to him. Don't they ever notice this contradiction?

18 October

Created in God's image, humans are inhabited by an entity that is an emanation of God – their higher self. But this divine entity does not reside within their physical body. If it did, it would perform wonders.

Depending on a person's degree of evolution, their higher self makes contact with their brain more or less often and for a varying length of time. But as for the moment, no human brain is ready to withstand the power of its vibrations and attune with it, the higher self does not linger. For yet a long time to come, and provided we give it the right conditions, it will have to work on our brain from a distance in order to prepare it. Our higher self will only take full possession of our brain the day our brain can accommodate it.

19 October

When we say that a man or a woman is a saint, we generally think of their qualities such as goodness, patience, self-sacrifice, and forgiveness of offenses. These are the qualities of a heart that harbours no selfish or aggressive feelings – a pure heart. However, true holiness belongs to a higher realm, that of intelligence enlightened by divine light. That is why only the spirit is holy. According to cabbalistic tradition, God is called 'the Holy One'. How many times, instead of saying 'God', do cabbalists use the expression 'the Holy One, Blessed be He'! And in the book of Revelation, the seraphim who stand before the throne of God never cease repeating day and night 'Holy, holy, holy, the Lord God the Almighty.'

It is important to distinguish between purity and holiness. Purity is the condition of holiness: to reach the holiness of the spirit, one must first have purified one's heart.

20 October

When humans are disappointed by events or dissatisfied with their fate, they tend to project themselves into the future. Hope is without doubt what they abandon last. But while waiting for better days, we need to find something to lean on in order to stand firm. Yet in order to stand firm, not only do we need faith, we must also maintain life inside us, and it is thanks to love that we maintain life. Otherwise, hope may be nothing but a flight from reality, and then it too will abandon us one day.

But what do humans generally do? At the slightest disappointment or when faced with the slightest obstacle, they lose their love, they lose faith, and then hope leaves them too. How can they be made to understand that difficulties are only overcome by faith, hope and love? But only on condition this hope, faith and love are turned towards God. These three virtues can be compared to the three faces of a crystal prism, and the divine presence is the ray of sun that falls upon this prism and is split into seven colours.

21 October

How many times have you had a feeling of emptiness – a feeling that something is missing? But instead of going out more, or asking yourself what new object to acquire or what prestigious situation to vie for, think rather of changing something about your perceptions. Cultivate the faculty of experiencing subtle sensations, and you will be able to spend centuries contemplating the sun, the stars, flowers, faces and so forth without ever losing interest.

Today, ads in the newspaper, on the radio and on television try to convince people that if they buy everything on show, they will feel fulfilled. No, listen to the spiritual Masters instead who tell you, 'Raise yourselves up on high through thought and prayer, and you will capture a particle, an imperceptible atom that will give you the taste for things.' As soon as you receive it, this atom will produce such intense and subtle vibrations within you, that you will awaken to a much vaster, richer life, and you will feel fulfilled.

22 October

***O**ne wonders where humans' fascination with gold comes from. Perhaps they vaguely sense it originates from sunlight which is so vital to their life. The truth is, there is a relationship between gold and light on every plane, for light is spiritual gold. Just as gold is the symbol of material wealth, so too is light the symbol of spiritual wealth.

The day humans understand what light truly is and learn to appreciate it, they will no longer exhaust themselves in the often disappointing and sometimes deadly pursuit of this very precious metal – gold. Some may feel drawn towards the sun's light, but since they still have a long way to go before managing to free themselves from matter's grip, they don't think any further than the metal.

23 *October*

*T*he seraphim govern the four principles of matter – earth, water, air and fire. It is they who reign at the top of the heavenly hierarchy, in the sephira of *Kether*. However, when we humans address the angels of the four elements, we only reach the servants of these four sublime beings. There must be no confusion – only the seraphim are the true fire, air, water and earth; they are inaccessible, and when they decide to manifest themselves, they do so through their servants.

If it so happens that one or more of the four elements unleash themselves on our planet, it is often humans themselves who are to blame: through their actions, but also through their thoughts, feelings, and disorderly behaviour, they constantly upset the forces of nature that eventually intervene to restore order. Why can't they understand that nothing they do is without consequence? Nature is not something inert and insensitive – it is alive and conscious, and whenever humans go beyond the limits of what it can accept, it reacts.

24 October

*T*he notion of the incarnation of children into a family is much more complex and profound than is generally thought. From time to time, upon staring deeply into their children's eyes, truly sensitive parents might feel as if they were offering their hospitality to unknown visitors for a while. This soul that has come to live with them was not of their creation, they are only giving it shelter on the physical plane.

Parents must be attentive and good to the soul they welcome and never forget that its true parents are its divine parents. Just like parents on earth who place their child in boarding school, the divine parents know that they owe something to those who have taken care of this child; and if it has been well-cared for, educated and loved, they reward them generously.

25 October

*E*very day, humans must engage in multiple occupations that force them to descend into matter. But they must only descend, not fall – the distinction must be clear. To avoid falling, they must remain connected to the spirit that dwells within them. Thus, when they go through internally difficult times, they will find the means to escape doubt, anguish and discouragement: stairs and ladders will provide them access to the higher regions of consciousness.

In matter, one can find all that is good, but also all that is bad. To avoid becoming engulfed, one must take care to descend without blocking the stairs, without breaking the ladders, without sawing the ropes, so as to be able to climb back up quickly and take shelter in the event of danger. Faith and a high ideal are the stairs, ladders and ropes that make it possible to climb back up quickly to the higher levels.

26 October

*E*verything that you ardently wish for is immediately realized on the subtle planes. And if you persist in your desires, these realizations that as yet only exist in the unseen, will descend further and further and take shape on the physical plane. Whether for good or for evil, all desires eventually come to pass in some way. Therefore, you must only concern yourself with the nature of these desires, so that in coming true, they do not lead you to make serious mistakes.

You may wish to become rich, but then imagine yourself sharing this wealth with all those in need, and not just using it for your own satisfaction. You may desire beauty, but not the type of beauty that troubles hearts: focus on spiritual beauty, beauty that inspires people and propels them towards the divine world. Whatever your wishes and your projects, endeavour to never lose sight of the moral side, otherwise, you too will suffer one day.

27 October

*E*very day, try to prepare the best inner conditions in order to be awake, available and active when you have the opportunity to attend an important event or make a life-changing encounter: meeting a being, meeting beauty, meeting a truth. Someone who has indulged in inferior activities or states that have drained them of their energies is not ready to fully live such encounters: inwardly, it is as if they are faced with a closed door.

To a certain extent, such situations can occur every day. Suppose that you are upset or in a bad mood, and then quite unexpectedly, you have to take action or receive an important guest. As a result, you are not able to present yourself with the proper expression and state of mind, and so it will not go as well as it could have, had you been well disposed. Even though you are there physically, you are unable to participate in the event with full awareness, because you have allowed your psychic energies to dissipate. You can only retain this energy if you are always careful to lead a harmonious life.

28 October

When a conflict arises between two people, they instinctively tend to refer to a third party, or else to a higher authority who must find a solution upon which they can agree, and this, as a rule, is the role of courts of law. If two people end up in court, it is because they have not been able to solve their problems on their own – those they have with each other, but also those they have with themselves. Because most often, the problems we have with others are the result of the ones we first and foremost have with ourselves.

We can only resolve our problems, and especially our inner problems, by focusing on a third and higher authority. It is this highest, most powerful authority that we call God, and we must, therefore, strive to reach him. God is the light within us, he is unity, and when we make the effort to rise all the way up to him, our inner tensions subside, currents harmonize, and we are reconciled with ourselves and with others.

29 October

When you have a migraine, a pimple, indigestion, and so on, do not always try to rid yourself of it immediately by taking medicine. It may indeed be that nature has given you this ailment in order to push you to do work on the psychic plane that you have never done before and would not otherwise do. So start by praying and concentrate on light while trying to forget this problem; after a while, not only may it take leave of you, but you will have made great progress internally.

Do not misunderstand me: I am not saying that prayer and thought are a cure for all ills and replace all medicine. I am only saying that instead of always choosing the easy way to get rid of the least discomfort through external means – tablets and pills – try to first draw upon a spiritual element, work with light, love, harmony and purity. Then, not only might you be able to free yourself from this slight inconvenience, your entire being will benefit, because the work that you so do not only affects a few cells somewhere in your body, but your whole physical and psychic being. And if you then take medication, remember that the efforts of thought will increase its positive effects.

30 October

***H**umans are drawn to money because they instinctively feel that it represents all the possibilities life has to offer. Only, they mistakenly confuse money and life. Just as life provides everything, they believe that money too will provide them with everything, and so they grant it an importance they are unable to give to life. They tremble at the thought their money might be stolen from them, and take extraordinary measures to protect it. Look at banks – they have become veritable fortresses. Nothing is better guarded and protected than their safes. But why don't humans tremble as much at the thought of wasting their life, which is their most precious asset because it is the quintessence of God himself? This quintessence contains all the wealth of the universe, and yet they accept to lose this wealth in pursuit of a few trinkets.

Yes, money is the material expression of all the possibilities life gives us, but only the material expression. We must learn to transpose it onto other planes: emotional, mental, and spiritual, in order to obtain the equivalent wealth on these planes.

31 October

*T*hroughout the ages, those who have guided the people had to begin by teaching them justice. This was already progress, and that is what Moses did. When Jesus came, he said that there was something greater than justice – mercy, forgiveness. But we must not stop there either, because forgiveness alone does not solve anything.

Of course we must forgive, but if someone comes to attack you, is it forbidden to be stronger than them? Be stronger than your enemy, and with a gesture, a look, a divine vibration, make them feel not so much your own superiority, but the superiority of the spirit – that is the ambition you should have. Just how long this will take is another matter. But at least work towards it, so as not to constantly be torn between the tendency to retaliate with violence and the tendency to allow yourself to be mistreated. True Christians must be armed, but armed with new weapons. If they are attacked, they must defend themselves, but using only these true weapons – love and light.

1 November

*T*hose people who, while they were alive, never acknowledged the reality of life after death or were only attached to material possessions roam about in the lower regions of the astral plane for a long time when they leave earth. They are wandering souls, who suffer, and although spirits of light try to help them, they still cannot break their attachments.

Those, on the other hand, who have cherished a great spiritual ideal during their life rapidly leave their body and fly away to the sublime regions, where they swim in light and joy. From there, they can send blessings to all those they have left below, to help and protect them. But they never come back to visit them, the way many people imagine. From the moment they leave their body, they are a long way from earth and do not come down again.

2 *November*

*T*he living are allowed to want to carry on relating to the dead, but not just anyhow. When someone dies, the doors of the earth close behind them; they find themselves in the grip of a new current of forces, and they do not have the right to go back. This is why we should avoid clinging to the dead and accompanying their departure with regrets, tears and wailing. So long as they have not passed the regions of the astral and mental planes, the distress of the living is a torment for them.

It is only when the dead reach the causal plane that nothing can disturb them anymore: it is as if they are in the centre of a magic circle of light, and no appeal or begging from the living can enter this circle if they do not want it to. It is good to pray for the dead, to think of them with love, to send them light so that they may find peace and become free, but we must not cling to them.

3 November

*T*he way people eat says a lot about how evolved they are. If they do not respect the food that daily gives them life, who will they respect? The food they take in is already blessed by the Creator, and the fact that it gives them life is precisely the greatest proof that it is blessed. God is in the food in the form of life, so it does not need to be blessed by humans to receive life.

You will say, 'But what is the point then of the words of blessing people traditionally say before meals?' A blessing is a kind of magic ritual – each word spoken contains vibrations that have the power to act on matter. The words of blessing prepare the food to be in harmony with those who are about to eat it: they create a connection and adaptation in their subtle bodies, so that they are already more receptive to all the treasures of divine life contained in the food.

4 November

*M*any people, when they are overwhelmed by difficulties and hardships, suddenly realize the mistakes they have made, due to neglect, ignorance or weakness, and they say to themselves, 'If only I had known...' They could have known, because at a certain point they were given all the right conditions for learning and working. But spiritual life requires efforts they were not prepared to make, and they neglected these good conditions. Other activities and preoccupations seemed more important at the time, and they were taken by surprise.

But whatever mistakes you have made, do not waste time feeling bad about it, and above all do not become discouraged. The worst thing is not making mistakes; it's telling yourself that your spiritual ideal is unachievable and discouraging, and then giving up. It is never too late to take up the path of light again. Once more you will soon be given other conditions. Try not to let them slip by!

5 November

*S*ometimes you meet people who imagine that giving themselves up to vague mystical impulses will attract the Holy Spirit. No, if you are to receive the gifts of the Holy Spirit one day, you must absolutely not give yourself up or, rather, you may do so but only after you have carried out a huge inner work of purification and self-mastery.

Whenever we want to tackle anything, we always have to begin by preparing the right conditions, and the first of these is to do some cleaning. When you need to pour liquid into a container, you check that the container is clean, and if it is dirty you wash it. So, how can anyone whose inner state resembles a dirty container believe that the Holy Spirit will come and live in them? What will come are dark, impure entities, because they will be attracted by the food that is there for them: all those feelings and thoughts inspired by the person's lower nature that they have been unable to master.

6 November

*T*here is always something suspect about the attitude of supposedly virtuous people who judge that 'sinners' must be rejected by God without being able to find his grace again. Over the centuries, these narrow-minded, fanatical people have used religion to condemn and persecute those who, according to them, have not behaved irreproachably. Some have even gone as far as inventing hell, into which the damned (damned, according to them!) are hurled, to suffer eternal punishment and be forever deprived of the presence of God and of his love. But that is not the truth.

God has placed a spark in all human beings – their spirit. This spark is a part of himself, and its presence in them means that they are a part of his nature. If they are to blame for anything, of course they deserve to be reprimanded and even punished. But even if they have to be treated severely and kept apart from others for a time, we must never forget that somewhere deep down inside them a divine seed exists and that this divine seed must be respected by everyone.

7 November

*K*nowledge, as a faculty, is not located in the brain alone, as is generally believed – we learn, we understand, we draw conclusions and we know. No, the brain's faculty of understanding and knowing is a synthesis of the properties of all our organs' cells – the cells of our heart, lungs, stomach, liver, sex organs, arms, legs and so on. Each cell in our body possesses a tiny intelligence that allows it to execute a specific task in the organ it belongs to, and the brain synthesizes all these intelligences. If the cells have reduced capacity, the brain remains obtuse. Everything is linked; we shouldn't separate the brain from the rest of the body. This is why, day after day, we must remember to bring purity, life and light to the cells of every one of our organs, so that they work well and this will be reflected in our brain.

The only purpose of the exercises given in our teaching – about how to breathe, eat, even wash, walk, sleep and so on – is the regeneration of our cells, so that we can broaden and deepen our understanding.

8 November

*I*f you open a seed and look at it under the microscope, you won't find the image there of the tree it will produce once you have planted it. How does it end up producing this huge creature with its roots, trunk, branches, leaves, flowers and fruits? In the same way, no observation under the microscope of the 'seed' a man gives to a woman can show what the child will be like. But once this seed has been sown in the mother's womb and nourished by her blood, it develops, and one day the child comes into the world possessing all its own physical and psychic traits.

We see this natural phenomenon endlessly being repeated before our eyes, revealing the mystery of human beings, the mystery of their psychic and spiritual life. For, they too possess an inner diagram, an original imprint, according to which the forces circulating within them are determined and directed. And in the same way that the seed is destined to become like its father, the tree, so human beings are called to strive for the perfection of their heavenly Father: this perfection is written into their structure.

9 November

*E*ach day, the coexistence of our two natures, the higher and the lower, pose such problems for us! This is why, when our higher nature encourages us to behave honestly, to make an effort, we must also make sure that our lower nature is not informed of it, so that it doesn't come and throw up obstacles. This is a principle used in military strategy: the generals who finalize the battle plans do not disclose them to everyone, because if the enemy knew of them they would prepare a counterattack. In the same way, when the higher nature makes its plans, it has to protect them from the lower nature's manoeuvring.

The lower nature mustn't be aware of what the higher nature is doing, but the higher nature, on the contrary, must keep watch over the lower nature to avoid its traps, since the lower nature is constantly busy fomenting shady business. So, it is necessary to keep our higher nature constantly on alert, so that it can observe what is happening and intervene, when needed, to restore order.

10 November

*I*n ancient times, it was the tradition for some priests and priestesses to have only one function, which was to maintain a fire in the temples that must never go out. Fire, flame and light in sanctuaries evoke the presence of the Divine in the universe, but also in human beings. In humans this fire is love, which like the sun must burn ceaselessly in their heart, and it is fed by sacrifice.

What is sacrifice? A transmutation. Only those who know how to make sacrifices possess the secret of transmuting matter, which is the very condition of life. This transmutation of matter can only be made by fire, especially the spiritual fire of love. Life is only possible because of sacrifice, because of love. Everywhere, from stones to the stars, love sustains the structure of the universe; if love disappeared, even our body would crumble to dust. And it is thanks to love, thanks to the sacrifices humans make for one another, that families and nations are also able to survive. Love is the greatest force in the universe.

11 November

A religion is only a form the divine spirit takes to manifest itself. But no form can remain unchanged. Christianity, which was born in the Middle East, took on certain elements in the beginning from Greek and Roman cultures. These elements were added to those inherited from the Jewish religion, which had itself been influenced by the religions of neighbouring countries: Egypt, Mesopotamia and so on. A religion is never born from nothing; it receives certain elements from previous religions and itself transforms as it spreads further from its place of origin.

Although people always preserve and study the same sacred texts, the way they understand and experience these texts becomes more and more remote from what they are reading. Evolution is the law of life, which is why it is not reasonable to desperately try and perpetuate the form of any religion; we should only make sure that it is always alive with the spirit.

12 November

*W*hether physically or psychically, vigilance and attention are indispensable. Do you fail to pay attention? If so, you are going to make a clumsy movement, bump against an obstacle or fall over. Neither your knowledge, your fortune, nor your virtues will save you. Lots of remarkable people have been the victims of accidents brought about by their lack of attention! Criminals, because they are aware that they might be taken by surprise at any moment, are extremely vigilant, which is how they often avoid prosecution. So, why leave vigilance to criminals? Do you imagine that your innocence and goodwill will automatically attract divine protection? No, if you are negligent, nothing and nobody will keep you safe.

You might say, 'But if I trust in God, if I love him, he will protect me.' Certainly, but if you are not vigilant, even your love for God will not save you. He will say to you, 'So you love me? That's fine, but I am not here to guard you and your home.' Neither your love nor your good qualities can be an excuse for not being vigilant. And this is even truer on the psychic plane.

13 November

*T*hose who lead an irreproachable life feel no need to be involved in the life of others: they do not mistrust them or criticize or judge them. True purity does not concern itself with impurity. The pure are not interested in knowing who is living an impure life. And this is why they enlighten and purify beings with their emanations and their light, whereas those who hound others on the pretext of setting them on the right path often only tarnish them.

If only we knew what drives certain people to set themselves up as moralists and dispensers of justice! So often, they persecute in others the very weaknesses they refuse to see in themselves! They need to be a bit more perceptive. If they are seeking purity, as they claim to be, let them begin by working on their own thoughts, feelings and desires. When others sense something clear and light-filled emanating from them, perhaps they will allow themselves to be influenced. But in the meantime, they should be left alone!

14 November

Sages and spiritual Masters are not all-powerful, and they know this, which is why they deal only with those they feel are able and, above all, willing to progress. It is pointless getting indignant and saying that a spiritual Master should have enough love to deal with everyone's evolution. However great his love, unfortunately he can do nothing for those who feel fine as they are and refuse to improve their understanding and behaviour. If they are satisfied with their condition, no one will be able to persuade them to change.

Ask teachers, even the most patient and devoted ones, whether they can teach anything to children who remain obstinately closed to whatever they are teaching. Only when life shakes these children up will they understand everything they have lost by not wanting to be taught. It is the same with many adults: it is life that will shake them up and even break them into pieces, until they understand that they must be willing to become part of the movement of evolution.

15 November

The only thing that enables us to relate to the Creator, our heavenly Father, is our understanding of what true life is. Until then, we can only have approximate, superficial, and mistaken concepts of him. Instead of looking for God in themselves, in the life he has given them, people make do with what has been said about him. Then they discuss the pros and cons, they ask themselves questions, they wonder whether he exists or not, and they remain forever uncertain and build nothing. The only ones who will never again ask questions about the existence of God are those who allow life to spring up within them.

Life, divine life, exists outside us, but it also exists within us; we are steeped in it. Even if they are rare, we do meet beings on earth who have understood the value and the beauty of this life and are living it. The heavenly powers show those who seek true life where to find those beings who have found it, so that these beings may help them and take them along with them. Then, even in the midst of great difficulties, they will never feel really isolated or abandoned.

16 November

*T*he cells of the human body are constantly being renewed; each day old worn out cells are replaced by new ones. This process of renewal is spread over seven years. So, after seven years the body's cells have been replaced, but that does not mean that the person has become a new being. The cells possess in effect a kind of memory, which they transmit in the form of etheric imprints to the replacement cells. Thoughts, feelings and energies circulate on these imprints as if along well marked out grooves and circuits, and they inherit this memory. This is why most humans continue to think in the same way and repeat the same mistakes: the new cells are subject to the influence of the old memory.

Anyone who truly wants to change must change the memory in their cells; in other words, as the new cells replace the old ones they must do all they can to imbue them with more elevated thoughts and feelings. For, even if they receive a spiritual teaching, they will not change deep down until they put their inner world in order.

17 November

*T*he fact that the physical world exists for us, that we are able to see the sky, the sun and the earth, is thanks to this invisible principle within us that allows us to be aware of them through the physical organs, our eyes. If this invisible principle did not exist in us, our eyes would be of no use to us, as we would see nothing. The visible world is merely the shell, the husk, of the invisible world, without which we would know nothing of all that exists around us.

We do not see life, but we see the manifestations of life; we do not see thoughts and feelings, but we see them variously expressed through the actions and creations that spring from them. In the same way, the world we know represents only the condensed, secreted forms and clothing of the invisible Being that created the universe and continues to give it life. And what we see is always very little in comparison with what we do not see. Everything around us shows us the limits of what we see and the vastness of what we do not see.

18 November

When humans hurt us, it's not really them that are trying to harm us but bad entities that are using them. Then, these entities move on, and after they have made use of the next person to carry out their malicious plans, they leave that person too and go looking for someone else. It is possible that though this person appeared to be an enemy, once they have got rid of the entity, they may then seem different and even regret their actions, and they may not even remember what they did. So, it is not reasonable to harbour resentment indefinitely towards someone or to want to take revenge. If you attack back, they will do the same, and then it will spiral until neither of you understands anymore what's going on, with each accusing the other of having started hostilities.

You may say, 'So, it's spirits we have to fight... But how?' By cultivating qualities and virtues that will prevent them from having a hold over you. Even if they continue to pursue you, they will not catch you; the gains you will have made on the spiritual plane will form a kind of rampart around you.

19 November

*P*rayer is not limited to saying words. Why is it that very often when people pray they spontaneously join their hands together? When they use this gesture, they instinctively find the deep meaning of prayer: one hand represents the mind and the other the heart. For a prayer to be powerful, it has to come from the mind and from the heart, from thought and feeling, that is, from the two principles – the masculine and the feminine.

That doesn't mean that you have to bring your hands together physically when you pray. You can pray with or without joining your hands… and some people also pray with their hands open at face level, palms facing forward; like that, the arms and the head together form the Hebrew letter shin ש. You can pray in any posture; what counts is not the physical attitude but the inner attitude, the participation of thought and feeling. Nor are the words the most important thing when you pray. They are important, of course, but only if they are also brought to life by thoughts and feelings on the psychic plane.

20 November

A true spiritual Master recognizes the Divine in his disciples and in everyone who comes to him, and it is the Divine in them that he addresses. Beyond their appearance and their sometimes wretched condition, he sees souls and spirits wanting only to grow in beauty and in light, and it is these souls and these spirits that he loves. It is pointless preaching love for one's neighbours if it is not explained to people what they must love in them and how to love them.

When you see how so many people behave in daily life, you cannot love them, and it's even pointless trying. Someone may be selfish, bad and hateful, and then you are told that they are your neighbour, that you have to love them... It's impossible! In fact, it is so impossible that not only will you fail but, in making the effort to love this monster, you will also detest them even more. If you are to succeed in loving them, you have to go beyond appearances and concentrate on the divine spark that is living in them and may one day emerge.

21 November

*T*he expression 'odour of sanctity', which you hear sometimes, does mean something. There are saints, spiritual Masters, who have worked so much on themselves that their psychic bodies emanate real fragrance. These fragrances are picked up by beings of light in the invisible world, who then rush to breathe them in. In certain cases, it can even happen that particularly sensitive people may sense these fragrances emanating from their soul.

These fragrances also emanate from the soul of those beings who have learned to accept and overcome their suffering. So often, you hear people complaining or shouting in an outraged manner at the slightest disappointment, trouble or injustice! The suffering they feel is like a burning fire. But those who consciously accept and remain silent, knowing that through patience and love they are purifying matter in their inner being – those people are also preparing fragrances in their soul. This is why knowing how to suffer is one of the greatest kinds of knowledge there is, one of the highest manifestations of love.

22 November

*T*he true sage knows that humans are destined one day to return to their heavenly homeland. Even if they meet every form of evil on the road to this homeland, even if they become discouraged or doubt not just others but themselves too, they do not founder. In their heart and soul there remains inscribed the truth that God created humans in his own image and that this image contains the potential for all riches, all victories and all joys.

The sage has a philosophy and knowledge based on the relationship between God, the universe and humans. The word 'optimism' isn't suitable as a definition of this philosophy, given that it is often used in everyday life as a synonym for naivety. It is more precise to speak of hope, that is to say, the certainty that the future can always be better. Even if the present is not great, in the Creator's plans it is always the powers of life and goodness that will eventually triumph one day.

23 November

On the physical level everyone is more or less safe, and they generally know how to protect themselves. But psychically, it is a different matter. Very few people are aware that dark energy currents pass through the surrounding atmosphere. These currents are produced by all the negativity emanating from the human psyche – anger, rebellion, envy, hatred, the desire for revenge, and so on – and these currents feed the evil entities that inhabit space.

We are all exposed to these currents. So how should we protect ourselves? We must begin by watching our own thoughts, feelings and desires and daily making them fairer, nobler and more selfless, so that they are food for beings of light only. In this way, we create all the right conditions for these beings to come, and it is these beings that will watch over us and protect us.

24 November

*W*hy do humans have the ability to rebel against God? Because when he created them, he placed his own will inside them. God is all-powerful, but he wanted to collaborate with human beings, and he gave them freedom. He made them responsible. So, it is up to humans to know how to use their freedom. And the best way to use it is to dedicate one's life to opening up a pathway, so that the energy currents from the world above come down and act on the earth, transforming it and purifying it.

Even if nature is beautiful, behind this apparent beauty and harmony, mountains, valleys, rivers, oceans and even the soil we walk on are permeated by unhealthy, harmful fluids. These have been produced over many, many centuries by generations of creatures living in violence, anarchy and chaos. This is why it is necessary for people who are conscious of their responsibility to make up their mind and set to work to neutralize dark currents, which are the cause of so much disorder and misfortune.

25 November

*S*omeone may tell me they have read all my books. I congratulate them, as there are a lot. But I ask, 'Which ones have you reread?' They look at me a bit surprised and reply, 'None.' 'Well, now choose a few and reread them several times. Because what have you really retained from all the books you have read just once? The human brain is not able to retain essential truths immediately or to grasp their whole meaning. Over the years your consciousness develops. When you reread these books, the same truths will appear to you in a new light, and you will find them even more enriching.'

And it is the same with the great book of living nature. For thousands of years nature has been right there, presenting humans with the same phenomena and the same sights. But it is up to them to develop their consciousness so that they read this book in a way that is always fresh. Even if they are looking at the same countryside, the same sky, the same sea, they will see them differently each day, because something in their consciousness has changed. And this is even truer when they watch the sun rise in the morning. Repetition is one of the most powerful factors of evolution.

26 November

***P**eople are praised for their qualities of wisdom, intelligence, fairness, kindness or generosity. But they did not create these qualities; they received them through entities that have been given by God the task of manifesting his infinite wealth. Of course, they have to make an effort themselves to receive what the entities have to give them. They have to apply themselves to deserve to possess these qualities – but that is all; they cannot do any more.

Humans are mistaken when they imagine that what they possess originates with them, that they created it. In reality, they only have the ability to receive these gifts, and when they have received them they must try to increase them and become conductors for them, in other words allow others to benefit from them too.

27 November

Humans must stop thinking of God as a Being outside of them. They must even stop imagining that he is somewhere above, in the heavens, while they are here on earth, separated from him by immeasurable distances; they think this justifies all the mistakes they make. Since God created them, he is in them, the same way a father and mother are in the child they gave birth to. Just as we carry our earthly father and mother inside us, all the more reason that we also carry our heavenly Father and Mother. Many will say they don't sense them. It's quite simply that they are not looking for them.

If you use meditation and prayer to try to go deep within, you will discover this presence. You will also understand that nothing is more important than working to make this presence more and more alive within you. You will begin to read this presence like writing engraved on your heart, and this living writing, at the same time as protecting you, will lead you along the paths of light.

28 November

On the pretext that it is impossible to meet true living spiritual Masters, some people go to spiritualist meetings and ask questions of masters from the past so as to benefit from their light. Let them be under no illusions: it is not masters but entities from the astral world that will come and answer their questions. Those who truly desire light must instead study the teaching of these great beings from the past and then put it into practice.

And it is not necessary to take part in spiritualist meetings if you want to receive visits from beings from the invisible world. Wherever there are people filled with true spiritual aspirations who come together to meditate and pray, beings of light will come to visit them, even when not specifically called. These beings make no sound; they have nothing out of the ordinary to tell; they simply fill souls with light, peace and inspiration.

29 November

Each finger is like an antenna specially prepared for picking up influences from space. The thumb is linked to Venus, the index finger to Jupiter, the middle finger to Saturn, the ring finger to the Sun and the small finger to Mercury.

Remember to do this exercise occasionally: raise your hand to the sky, and focus on each finger's ability to attract the positive currents emitted by these planets. In this way, when you meet someone and shake their hand, or even if you only greet them from a distance, you will send them harmonious, life-giving waves of energy and rays of colour. Even when you do not speak to the people you meet, remember you can always have a positive influence on them.

30 November

Physical hunger is symbolic of all the appetites, of all greed. Humans feel driven to satisfy so many kinds of hunger. Hunger for pleasure, for power, for glory, for vengeance… their astral stomach is insatiable! And those who seek to satisfy all these hungers rarely realize that, instead of nourishing themselves, they are inwardly sacrificing something extremely precious – particles of divine life – for a few minutes of happiness.

If it were possible to place on one pan of a pair of scales what they have gained by satisfying all these desires, and on the other pan what they have lost by not trying to control themselves, they would see they have lost almost everything and gained very, very little. They never consider that sensations, even the strongest and most pleasant ones, fade and are forgotten (what they ate yesterday no longer counts for today), and so they are preparing a life of spiritual poverty and famine for themselves.

1 December

*T*here is no such thing as a place of eternal damnation for sinners, and what Christians call hell is a fabrication. Only purgatory exists, which, as the name implies, is the region where, for a greater or shorter length of time, humans 'purge themselves' of their faults, that is to say they wash and purify themselves – and this purification is obviously accompanied by suffering.

But human beings' evolution does not stop the moment they atone for their faults. Humans' true evolution takes place on earth. Since they did wrong on earth, they must return to earth to repair the damage they did there. For having regrets and suffering do not suffice, suffering does not mend the mistakes that were made. Humans must return to earth to repair their mistakes. There is no other explication for reincarnation. If humans had already atoned for their sins in the hereafter, why should they have to come back down to earth again? By law, they are obliged to mend their mistakes in all the regions of the universe where their mistakes caused disorder and destruction.

2 December

*T*he principle of life and the principle of death constantly manifest themselves throughout all of nature and, consequently, in human beings too. As soon as a foetus is formed within a mother's womb, the principle of death begins to fight against the principle of life. Its action is limited at first – it is the spirit that triumphs. But later on, once the spirit has succeeded in carrying out its projects within a person, it gradually leaves their body.

Everything that is born must die, this is a law. It is impossible to conquer the principle of destruction, but we are not obliged to submit to it. When old age is upon us, when we lose our strength and our physical means, we must tell ourselves that now, more than ever, is the time to seek out other activities. For there are always other tasks and other sources of joy for those who know how to dig deep within themselves in order to bring forth their spiritual energy, and this energy is boundless.

3 December

Since the universe was created by God, all of nature is the expression of divine harmony and perfection. Nowhere is this harmony and perfection better represented than in the human body. Everywhere else, this beauty is dispersed – the oceans, for instance, represent one part of the cosmic body; the rivers another; the mountains, the forests and the sky yet others. Only men's and women's bodies can express this beauty in its entirety.

God has summed up the whole of creation in men and women. That is why when a human body approaches this ideal of beauty – through its proportions and especially its emanations – initiates contemplate it with delight. They say to themselves, 'Here is a creature that is a perfect image of divine virtues'. But they do not stop there: in their contemplation of this being, they endeavour to find the splendour of the Creator.

4 December

*M*agic can be defined as the application of the laws of physics to the spiritual realm. One of these laws highlights the power of concentration. Using a magnifying glass, focus the sun's rays into a point on a sheet of paper – they will set it on fire. Similarly, spiritual physics teaches us that human thought has powers comparable to those of the sun's rays.

Those who have learned to strongly concentrate their thought on a given point can succeed in producing beneficial effects in the world. Even if we cannot see anything on the physical plane, in the etheric, astral and mental* realms, their thought can ignite a fire that will burn up many impurities.

* See note and diagram, p. 394 and 395.

5 December

Certain tendencies are deeply-rooted in human beings, while others must be constantly stimulated through education, by rules imposed upon them or that are self-imposed, as well as through studies and through prayer. Humans do not need to be prodded to satisfy their hunger, their taste for pleasure, their desire to dominate others and to possess more and more. These instincts are so deeply entrenched in them that even if they wish to resist them, it is very hard.

But when it comes to reasoning, to showing discernment, restraint and mastery, then encouragement and support are needed. This is explained by the fact that humans' instinctive nature, inherited from the animal kingdom, has for millennia had ample time to develop, to strengthen itself within them. Wisdom, on the contrary, which belongs to regions far removed from instincts, has only emerged recently in them, which is why it struggles to make its voice heard. But humans must turn to it each day, providing it with the conditions and the means to impose itself.

6 December

***P**hilosophers so often make up systems that only account for their personal view of the world. And all too often, this view, which is bound to be limited, is a reflection of their spiritual, psychic, intellectual, or even physical shortcomings. Not to mention those who, trying to be original, present nonsensical theories.

The truth is that there is only one system that explains the universe, one system that represents the Creator, creation and created beings; and philosophers must reflect deeply to try to retrace the foundations of this system. That they would then express the results of their research according to their own temperament and sensitivity – or one might say with their own voice – is only normal. When singers sing their part, they can only do so with their own voice, through which they express the depths of who they are. But they must still respect the score; they have no right to sing notes different from those written. Similarly, philosophers have no right to sing anything other than what is written in the great book of life – they are only entitled to use their own vocal chords.

7 December

We are used to opposing heaven and earth, yet heaven and earth are not two opposite or even separate worlds: not only are they in constant contact with one another, their exchanges sustain life in the universe.

Heaven and earth – or take even more concretely the sun and the earth. They too exchange continuously, but we only see the more material aspect of these exchanges – the sun's rays that shine down on us. We see nothing of all that also rises from the earth towards the sun. Yet some particularly sensitive people have been able to see entities descend from the higher regions to work on human beings, animals and stones, then leave once their work was done. There are extraordinarily poetic stories on this subject. One day, all of humanity will be able to behold the creatures that come and go between the earth and the sun, and even further still.

8 December

***H**umans are unaware that thoughts, feelings and deeds which are not inspired by true love and wisdom produce disturbances in the unseen, the effects of which extend well beyond their lives on earth. They themselves are no longer there, but any selfish and malevolent thoughts, feelings and actions they did not bother to repair add fuel to the destructive currents that flow through space and poison the earth's psychic atmosphere.

So try to realize that each of your manifestations not only produces effects on specific people, at a given time and place; they also trigger beneficial or evil forces in the invisible world, and we do not know just how far or for how long these forces will have the power to act. Consequently, take stock of yourselves from time to time. Recall the circumstances in which you could have behaved better, and if you cannot mend your mistakes materially, strive at least, by thought, to restore harmony and peace in and around you.

9 December

When contemplating the beauty and depth of certain works of art and of certain philosophical, initiatic, and mystical works, one realizes that their authors have beheld a distant and elevated reality that escapes ordinary consciousness. To gain access to this reality, not only did they have to cross through the opaque layers of physical matter, but also the hazy layers of psychic matter. Until then, what they believed to be reality was in fact only an appearance thereof, a distorted reflection, or at best, a veil that hid it from their view.

The goal of initiation is to lift a veil. This is the origin of the expression 'lifting the veil of Isis' passed down by tradition. In Isis, the great female figure of Egyptian religion, initiates saw a symbol of primordial Nature from which all beings and all the elements of creation issued forth, and they took her as their main object of study. In their desire to know her, they strive to seek and understand all of the existences she generates and through which she manifests herself, until they discover the ultimate reality.

10 December

*Y*ou all know the wonderful tales where the magician or the sorceress only has to utter a few words to conjure up a castle, or tables covered with the most delectable dishes, or a great bird on which to travel through space and so forth. These stories are not pure inventions, they have meaning – they remind us of a time long ago when humans possessed the magic word. But little by little, as they sunk down into matter, humans lost their power over it, and were no longer able to master it. Every day, people must grapple with matter so as to shape it, draw subsistence from it, find shelter and make the objects they need, and it constantly offers up resistance.

In reality, the power of the Word has not been definitively taken away from humans, and they are capable of finding it again, provided they undertake a great work of inner transformation. We can define the Word as the synthesis of all expressions of psychic life. This work of transformation therefore begins with the mastery of thoughts, feelings and desires.

11 December

*E*ven if human beings aren't aware of it, all of them come to earth with the imprints of what they experienced in the heavenly regions with God. This life is recorded within them as an indelible memory, which is why they sometimes feel nostalgia for it. Sometimes, an encounter, a face, a reading, a landscape, an image, or music awakens a distant memory within them. They again experience a few moments of paradise, they feel inhabited by peace and light. Unfortunately, it doesn't last; and when the time comes to resume their daily activities, they fail to realize that there is something they could do to retain these states, and they even forget them.

Far from God, far from the spiritual sun, humans gradually lose every opportunity to live and manifest themselves with joy, love and freedom. They could very easily lead their earthly lives and fulfil their obligations and still maintain their bond with him. But this obviously requires a lot of vigilance and, when they feel they are drifting away, they must do everything to find their way back.

12 December

Why do invocations to God or to the gods hold such a great place in all religions? Because the most powerful way to get in touch with an entity is to speak its name; the vibrations of this name enable us to rise up to it. Taking an example from everyday life, we can say that speaking a name is like dialling a telephone number: we are put through to the person we called. Even if we don't know what shape or what features the entity we invoke may have, it doesn't matter – it is enough to know its name. If we utter it with a pure heart and the awareness of what it represents in the divine world, this name becomes a genuine magical power.

A name reflects the entity that bears it. Those who meditate on God's name and invoke it, immersing themselves in the holiness of the light, are filled with his emanations, and they sanctify all the creatures and objects they approach.

13 December

People may attack you without even knowing why, just as you too may fail to understand why you are attacking them. This is because humans are often the unconscious instruments of dark forces that have seized hold of them. To protect ourselves from humans, we must first learn to protect ourselves from the evil spirits that come to inhabit them, for behind every physical enemy, a dark entity is always at work.

The battles we must wage to defend ourselves are therefore of a very subtle nature. We must leave enemies alone, without seeking to harm them, rather only training ourselves internally, strengthening ourselves, cultivating qualities of purity, kindness and patience, so as to attract the help of the entities of light. Upon their arrival, they will drive out the dark entities that use our enemies to harm us, and they will settle in their place. Then, one day, the very people who acted as adversaries will behave like friends.

14 December

*T*he universe was created by two principles – the masculine principle and the feminine principle – and it can only subsist through the work of both these principles. Contained within the number 2 are all the possibilities for creation, but so too are all the possibilities for division, and as such, confrontation. The number 2 is also the beginning of what is called evil, which is why it is said that 2 is the number of initiation. All the deepest, most complex, most dangerous questions are contained within the number 2. It even harbours the secret of the existence of the so-called devil always described as an entity that rears up against God, declaring himself as his adversary.

In reality, God has no adversary. Since he is the 1, he is beyond good and evil. God is not only the good, he is also not opposed to the devil, the embodiment of evil and whom he cannot defeat. Both good and evil are his servants.

15 December

*A*s churches and temples are holy places where multitudes of people have already gathered to pray, you will find good conditions to pray there. But the most important element is you. Introduce order, purity, and light within you and wherever you are, your prayer will rise up to the throne of God.

And just as it is not necessary to enter a place of worship to worship God, neither is there necessarily a time. Each religion has chosen a particular day for worship. But in reality there is no difference between these days. In the eyes of God, every day is equally sacred and blessed. It makes no sense to spend six days in prosaic pursuits and activities, then on the seventh, finally remember that God exists and turn our gaze to him. In what state will you come before him if you have lived negligently and unconsciously the six other days? What you experience on the seventh day depends on how you have lived the previous six. It is therefore everywhere and every day that we must feel like we are in the temple of God to celebrate and adore him.

16 December

*W*hen you need to use an object, remember to handle it gently. For in a way, all objects are alive, and they retain what happens around them. They are like a photographer's sensitive plates: they could be made to tell many of the events they have witnessed.

Even if it is hard for you to accept, embrace the idea that all the objects you touch become imbued with your emanations. In every room of the house in which you live, there are thus objects covered with layers that are good or bad conductors of light from the world on-high. And if hateful thoughts and feelings, malicious words and evil looks are cast upon these objects, they also become like magnets: they attract the evil currents that circulate through space. Consequently, be attentive so that through your words, thoughts, and feelings, the objects around you become magnets that will attract only light, joy, beauty, and even health, spreading them all around you.

17 December

O*ur entire being is like a cup that we must wash and purify in order to receive divine foods, nectar and ambrosia. We hear people complaining that they have long held their cup up to the Lord for him to fill with his blessings, and are astonished not to have received anything – their cup remains empty. But what are they thinking? What can the Lord pour into a cup that has not been washed?*

The Lord, who is very wise, knows that it would be pointless and even harmful if he were to pour his life and his light, into human beings who have not purified themselves. The resulting mixture would be indigestible, toxic, and their psychic body could not handle it. For their safety, it is better that their cup remain empty so long as they have not washed themselves.

18 December

***H**umans are merciless towards animals: they use any means to exploit them, and they do not hesitate to slaughter them to satisfy their needs and interests, or even just for their enjoyment. Animals, for their part, are wary of humans: they run from them, and if they feel threatened, they attack.

However, it is said that there are cases where the light and love that emanate from some beings tame even wild animals, because animals have a certain sense. This sense allows them to judge humans – often even better so than humans who lack discernment and intuition. This is why the misunderstanding and hostility between humans and animals cannot last indefinitely. If humans can manage to live together as brothers, they will also make peace with animals. We will no longer speak of wild animals and tamed animals, both will once again be brothers of humankind.

19 December

*E*ach religion has its own language, its own form of expression, but they all speak of the day when, after having distanced themselves from God, humans return to him, for within him lies their origin. They tell different stories to explain this distancing and this return, they use different expressions and images, but it is always about the same reality.

Humans have distanced themselves from God, but even if in doing so they made mistakes, this distancing occurred with his consent. God could have refused humans this freedom, but in his infinite love, not only did he leave them free to distance themselves from him, he also gave them the possibility to come back to him. Initiatic science teaches the methods that allow humans to regain possession of their spiritual bodies, to return to paradise, their heavenly homeland. And this paradise is foremost found within them.

20 December

*I*n their psychic life, just as in their physical life, human beings are subjected to alternations. For a time they feel happy, complete and full of hope. But it doesn't last, and suddenly, they enter into a period of darkness, of deprivation, without always understanding why.

On earth, we cannot inwardly live in eternal spring, in the midst of flowers and song birds; at some point winter is bound to come. But we are not obliged to suffer through it, we can prepare for it by making provisions, and not spending everything we have gathered during the period of plenty. When we feel good inside and everything seems easier, we have a tendency to become careless. On the contrary, this is the time to be vigilant, far-sighted, and to put certain provisions aside: the period of scarcity – winter, symbolically – will be less difficult to weather. We mustn't forget: since it is always the difficult times that force us to progress, this period will come, and it is wise to set aside reserves to help overcome them.

21 December

*T*he sun, which looks the same to us each day, is in fact always new: at every moment, its emanations and its radiations are different. It is the life, the content that is at all times new. When you are able to go far and high enough, beyond the container, beyond the forms, in order to penetrate the content, that is to say the life, you will find that everything is new – heaven and earth are constantly new!

So many riches, so many wonders are right in front of people's eyes, but they have yet to see them because their consciousness is obscured, it stagnates too low down. But the day they reach a higher level of consciousness, they will discover what in reality has always existed, and what they had never seen before. Every day of the year, the sun shines above them, but they have not yet seen it until they rejoice in its presence, and feel that it is a living, intelligent being, with which they can establish a relationship.

22 December

I*f* humans are not able to go into the mountains with a proper state of mind, they disturb the pure and luminous entities living there. So, one day, these entities go elsewhere, to spots no one can easily reach. Once a place has been deserted by these entities, it loses its sacred nature, and is no longer as imbued with spiritual force. Those who then come to visit these places no longer receive anything and return home just as poor and as limited as before.

What is the use of trying so hard to climb mountain slopes if you do not understand that the ascent of physical mountains is an image of the ascent of spiritual mountains? Climbers must feel that they are ridding themselves of all that encumbers them and that weighs them down, until they feel divine order penetrate within them. They meet with silence, and in this silence they discover the origin of things, they unite themselves with the First Cause and they melt into the ocean of cosmic light.

23 December

*I*n the sacred texts, bread is often the symbol of spiritual food: that which we receive from heaven, but also that which we are able to give. All the good things prepared by our heart, our intellect, our soul and our spirit are like bread that we must not let lower entities eat, but keep safely for angels and heavenly entities. So many visitors from the divine world would be happy to stay amongst us, but they cannot remain in just any conditions. If, when they arrive, they find that they were not expected and that dark entities have already eaten everything that should have been used to feed them, they move on.

Take this truth seriously. Tell yourselves that spirits of light come down to visit humans every day. They are visitors bearing gifts, but we must at least be able to welcome them with food they appreciate: thoughts and feelings inspired by the need to grow increasingly more in the light. Otherwise, they will leave, because they do not want to starve and they will never accept to nourish themselves with impurities.

24 December

*T*o celebrate Christmas is to prepare ourselves for the birth of the cosmic principle of Christ in our soul. For Christ, which is a cosmic principle, can be born within us just as it was born within Jesus.

The birth of Jesus was undoubtedly an historic event of the utmost importance, but it was not necessary to insist so much on this event with the belief that it changed the course of history: the birth of a human being at one point in time does not change very much. If it was enough for Jesus to have been born two thousand years ago, why has the kingdom of God not yet come to earth? War, famine and misery should have all disappeared. Real transformations can only be brought about by a great number of people who have made the birth of Jesus an internal, spiritual event: the birth of Christ within them. We will be able to say that the birth of Jesus truly changed the course of history when Christians are able to manifest themselves everywhere as bearers of light and peace.

25 December

*T*here is no historical certainty about the circumstances of Jesus' birth. However, if according to tradition, he was born in a cave or in a stable, on straw, and not in a dwelling worthy of his mission like a palace or a temple, it is because the story of this birth is symbolic. Do not be surprised if I tell you that this cave in which the divine child must be born is also in our body – it corresponds to a spiritual centre located approximately 4 cm below the navel. This centre, which the Japanese call 'Hara' – the word for belly – has an important role to play in spiritual life. This is the cave where the Christ must be born.

Did you perhaps think that Christ could only be born in your head? Yet have you ever seen a child born from its mother's brain? The belly and the bowels are not generally considered as noble parts of the body, but this is the very place the Creator has chosen for the perpetuation of humanity. And it is here too that we must bring forth this new consciousness: the Christ Child.

26 December

Place within your head, your heart and your soul, a sublime ideal, an ideal that you may never attain. And do not think that the pursuit of such an ideal is discouraging. On the contrary. Observe yourselves: how do you feel when you get what you want? For a moment you are satisfied, but then what? As soon as you no longer have to make an effort to reach a new goal, you lose your drive and sometimes, even, your taste for life. So, set yourselves a goal that you will never reach and you will always remain alert, active, and enthusiastic.

Human beings have infinite possibilities in their thoughts and desires; they have no limits in the world of the soul and the spirit. If they feel limited, it is because they have limited themselves. You must therefore be able to nourish an unattainable ideal consciously: little by little, you feel that thanks to your desires and your thoughts, you are able to rise very high in space; there, you touch beings and elements in exact correspondence with these desires and thoughts, and you draw them to you, you nourish yourselves with them.

27 December

***H**umans wear their body, they live with it, they take care of it, they feed it, they wash it, they dress it and they even put make-up on it, but they do not bother to decipher what their body, with its limbs and its organs, wants to tell them. They would do best to study how Cosmic Intelligence thought of things by putting their body at the service of their intellect, their heart, and their will; they will understand that they must draw inspiration from this lesson for the conduct of their inner life, and they will know how to put all that is materiel and ephemeral in service of this eternal principle, their spirit.

Materiel and ephemeral things inevitably have a role to play in our life; but for this role to be beneficial, we must involve them in the activity of the spirit. It is not enough to multiply encounters, information, knowledge, or adventures, even if, in the moment, it gives us the feeling of living fully. It is not 'in the moment' that counts; it is the assessment we make of our life years later. That is why it is useful to review our choices and activities from time to time, and ask ourselves, 'What does all this really bring me?'

28 December

When God created human beings, he laid in them the seeds of all the qualities and virtues as well as all the gifts. They are there, still dormant, and to develop them, humans must first use their thought, then vivify this thought with feelings, and finally put their will to work to achieve what they thought and felt. Therefore, it is like a call to spiritual entities that are very far away, very high up, and these entities respond to their call by coming to manifest themselves through them.

Whatever qualities and gifts humans manage to develop, they owe it to the sacrifices of entities from the spiritual world. They make these sacrifices with joy. But to fully benefit from them, humans must be conscious and grateful. Grateful how? By striving to be attentive, kind and generous to the creatures around them – not only humans but also animals and plants and all of creation. These entities ask for nothing more. We must have something to offer to all the visible and invisible beings that help us to live and grow: a joy, a look, a ray.

29 December

*T*he further we progress along the path of truth, the freer we become. We must therefore strive to climb higher and higher. However, true freedom is found only at the summit, in God. This is why, for human beings as for any other creature in the universe, absolute freedom does not exist. Only the Creator is absolutely free. No creature is totally free, not even the angels and archangels; they are immersed in the soul of the Lord, they are the instruments of his will, and as such, are not entirely free. They are free within the Lord's freedom, but not free in relation to him. Only the Lord is free, and the closer creatures draw to the Lord, the freer they become within his freedom, but not otherwise.

It is therefore at the highest level, on the divine plane, that the word 'freedom' takes on its full meaning. When we fulfil the will of God, he manifests himself in us, and we ourselves become free because of his freedom. It is his presence within us that sets us free. It is thanks to his freedom of action that we are alive.

30 December

If humans do not know how to act today, what future do they think they can expect? While hoping it will be better, in truth they are worried: what to do to be safe from need, from danger? For it is true that the future is always uncertain. It is therefore pointless to waste time and energy worrying about all the accidents that might happen and the ways of protecting ourselves. Whatever the events, the only way to find solutions for the future is to do the best job we can today.

The present can therefore be defined as the means of remedying the mistakes of the past and of creating the future. People who always postpone the efforts to be made, never know the future, they stagnate in an endless past. As long as the present remains the same as the past, the future can only be an extension, an amplification of the past. For those who are lazy and neglectful, the past lingers on, whereas for those who are conscious and active, the present works on the past and prepares a future of light and joy.

31 December

Since human beings represent a microcosm, a reflection of the macrocosm, all constellations exist within them too. Not only is each one related to a part of their physical body, but they also exist within them in the form of tendencies and character traits. And just as the sun travels through the zodiac over the course of a year, we too can travel – via our spirit which is our sun – through the twelve constellations to benefit from their positive influences.

So, the twelve constellations are Aries – energy, audacity; Taurus – tenacity, patience; Gemini – intellectual abilities; Cancer – sensitivity, intuition about the invisible world; Leo – generosity, nobility; Virgo – purity, a love of order; Libra – balance, harmony; Scorpio – the sublimation of energies; Sagittarius – impetus toward the spiritual world; Capricorn – self-dominance, authority; Aquarius – universality, brotherhood; Pisces – sacrifice.

The Night of Wesak

*E*ach year, in the Himalayas, during the night of the full moon in May, the ceremony of Wesak takes place.*

The full moon in May is doubly under the influence of Taurus: the sun has been in this sign since 21 April, and the moon is also exalted in this sign.** Taurus represents prolific nature, fertility and abundance, emphasized further by the fact that it is the home of Venus, the planet of creation. So the full moon in May offers the best conditions for working with the forces of nature to attract heaven's blessings for the harvest and livestock, but also for human beings. For, if humans know how to attract the beneficial effects circulating through the cosmos at this time, they too can benefit from them, not only on the physical plane but also on the spiritual plane. This is why, by means of meditations, prayers, chants and magical invocations, initiates seek to create lines of force in space that will attract energies, which they send to all beings who are vigilant, awakened and capable of participating at this event.

* Wesak is the festival of the Buddha. In Tibet, it is celebrated in the valley of Wesak.

** Some years, when the sun is in Taurus, the full moon takes place in April.

There are places on earth that are more favourable than others for this cosmic work. The site where the ceremony of Wesak takes place is the most powerful of all. Some initiates go there physically, others by astral projection. But it is possible for everyone, including you, to take part in thought. During this night, you must not keep any metal object on you, since metal is not a good conductor of the waves of energy that come down from spiritual regions. But the only truly essential condition for being admitted to this festival is harmony. So be careful not to hold onto any negative thought or feeling towards others, and find the right inner attitude that will allow you to receive the blessings that the initiates send to the children of God on this night.

INDEX

A

B

D

G

H

I

J

M

N

O

P

Q

R

S

T

U

V

W

Y

Note: The three fundamental activities which characterize human beings are thinking (by means of the intellect or mind), feeling (by means of the heart), and doing (by means of the physical body). You must not believe that only the physical body is material; the heart and mind are also material instruments, but the matter of which they are made is far subtler than that of the physical body.

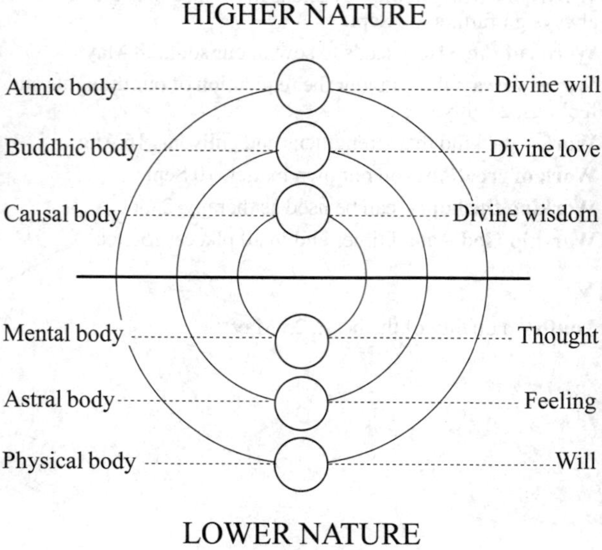

An age-old esoteric tradition teaches that the support or vehicle of feeling is the astral body, and that of the intellect, the mental body. But this trinity made up of our physical, astral, and mental bodies, constitutes our imperfect human nature, and the three faculties of thought, feeling, and action also exist on a higher level, their vehicles being respectively, the causal, buddhic, and atmic bodies which go to make up our divine self.

In the diagram, the three large concentric circles indicate the links which exist between the lower and the higher bodies. The physical body, which represents strength, will, and power on the material level, is linked to the atmic body, which represents divine power, strength, and will. The astral body, which represents our egotistical, personal feelings and desires, is linked to the buddhic body, which represents divine love. The mental body, which represents our ordinary, self-serving thoughts, is linked to the causal body, which represents divine wisdom.

(Man's Psychic Life: Elements and Structures, Izvor Collection No. 222, chap. 3)

Introduction to the Sephirotic Tree

Jesus said, 'And this is eternal life, that they may know you, the only true God'.

For those who aspire to know the Creator of heaven and earth, to feel his presence, to enter into his infinity and his eternity, it is necessary to have a deep understanding of a system that explains the world. The system that seemed to me to be the best, the most extensive and at the same time the most precise I found in the cabbalistic tradition – the sephirotic Tree, the Tree of Life. Its knowledge offers the deepest, most structured, overall view of what we need to study and work on.

The cabbalists divide the universe into ten regions or ten sephiroth corresponding to the first ten numbers (the word 'sephirah' and its plural 'sephiroth' mean enumeration). Each sephirah is identified by means of five names: the name of God, the name of the sephirah, the name of the archangel at the head of the angelic order, the angelic order itself, and a planet. God directs these ten regions, but under a different name in each one. This is why the Cabbalah gives God ten names, each corresponding to different attributes. God is one, but manifests in a different way in each region.

This Tree of Life is presented as a very simple diagram, but its contents are inexhaustible. For me it is the key that allows the mysteries of creation to be deciphered. It is not meant to teach us astronomy or cosmology, and anyway no one can say exactly what the universe is or how it was created. This Tree represents an explanatory system of the world that is by nature mystical. Through meditation and contemplation and a life of saintliness, the exceptional minds that devised it came to grasp a cosmic reality, and it is essentially their teaching that survives to this day, passed down by tradition and continually taken up and meditated on through the centuries.

A spiritual Master is conscious of the responsibilities he is taking by allowing humans to enter this holy sanctuary, and so when you approach this knowledge you must do so with much humility, respect and reverence. By returning often to this diagram, you will find lights being switched on inside you. You will certainly never manage to explore all its riches, but from Malkuth to Kether this representation of an ideal world will always draw you higher.

TREE OF LIFE

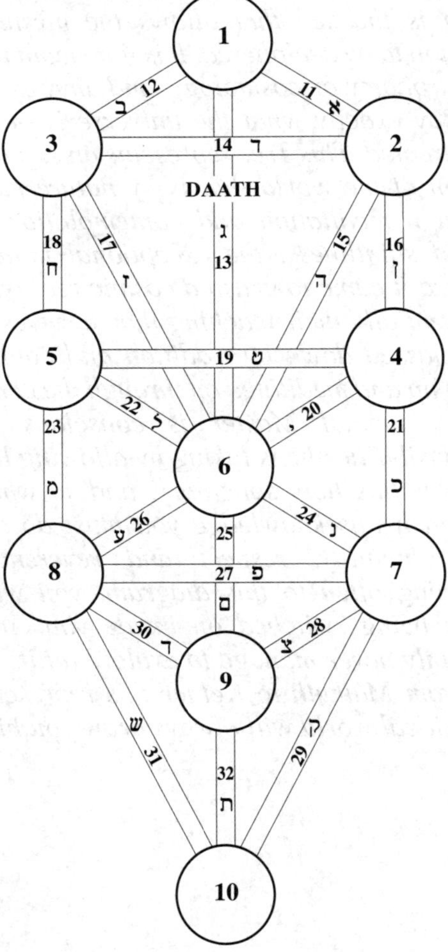
1
2
3
4
5
6
7
8
9
10
DAATH
11 א
12 ב
13 ג
14 ד
15 ה
16 ו
17 ז
18 ח
19 ט
20 י
21 כ
22 ל
23 מ
24 נ
25 ס
26 ע
27 פ
28 צ
29 ק
30 ר
31 ש
32 ת

TREE OF LIFE

1 Ehieh
Kether – *Crown*
Metatron
Hayoth haKadesch – *Seraphim*
Rashith haGalgalim – *First Swirlings (Neptune)*
♆

2 Yah
Chokmah – *Wisdom*
Raziel
Ophanim – *Cherubim*
Mazloth – *The Zodiac (Uranus)*
♅

3 Jehovah
Binah – *Understanding*
Tzaphkiel
Aralim – *Thrones*
Shabbathai – *Saturn*
♄

4 El
Chesed – *Mercy*
Tzsadkiel
Hashmalim – *Dominations*
Tzedek– *Jupiter*
♃

5 Elohim Gibor
Geburah – Severity
Kamaël
Seraphim – Powers
Maadim – Mars
♂

6 Eloha vaDaath
Tiphareth – *Beauty*
Mikhaël
Malakhim – *Virtues*
Shemesh – *Sun*
☉

7 Jehovah Tzebaoth
Netzach – *Victory*
Haniel
Elohim – *Principalities*
Noga – *Venus*
♀

8 Elohim Tzebaoth
Hod – *Glory*
Raphaël
Bnei-Elohim – *Archangels*
Kokab – *Mercury*
☿

9 Shaddai El Hai
Yesod – *Foundation*
Gabriel
Kerubim – *Angels*
Levana – *Moon*
☽

10 Adonai-Melek
Malkuth – *The Kingdom*
Uriel (Sandalfon)
Ishim – *Beatified Souls*
Olem Ha Yesodoth – *earth*
♁

Editor-Distributor

Editions Prosveta S.A. - F - 83601 Fréjus CEDEX (France)
Tel. (33) 04 94 19 33 33 – Fax (33) 04 94 19 33 34
www.prosveta.fr – www.prosveta.com
international@prosveta.com

** Publisher in his own language - ** Distributor - *** POS*

Distributors

AUSTRALIA
** PROSVETA AUSTRALIA – Port Kennedy WA 6172
Tel. (61) 8 9594 1145 – prosveta.au@aapt.net.au

CANADA
** PROSVETA Inc. – Canton-de-Hatley (Qc), J0B 2C0
Tel. (819) 564-8212 – Fax. (819) 564-1823
in Canada, call toll free: 1-800-854-8212
prosveta@prosveta-canada.com – www.prosveta-canada.com

CYPRUS
** THE SOLAR CIVILISATION BOOKSHOP. – 1305 Nicosie
Tél. 00357-22-377 503 – heavenlight@primehome.com - www.prosveta.com

GREAT BRITAIN – IRELAND
** PROSVETA – East Sussex TN 22 3JJ
Tel. (44) (01825) 712988 – Fax (44) (01825) 713386
orders@prosveta.co.uk – www.prosveta.co.uk

INDIA
* VIJ BOOKS INDIA PVT. LTD. *(Anglais et Hindi)* – New Dehli - 110 002
Tel. + 91-11-43596460, 011-65449971 – Fax +91-11-47340674
vijbooks@rediffmail.com – www.vijbooks.com
* BOOK MEDIA (Malayalam) – Kerala – www.indulekha.com/bookmedia
Tél. +91 94 47 53 62 40 – bookmediaindia@gmail.com

ISRAEL
* HADKEREN PUBLISHING HOUSE – P.O box 8426 – Tel-Aviv Jaffa 6108301
www.hadkeren.co.il – talya@hadkeren.co.il

LEBANON
** PROSVETA LIBAN – P.O. Box 90-995 – Jdeidet-el-Metn, Beirut
Tel. 961 (0) 3 448 560 – prosveta_lb@terra.net.lb – www.prosveta-liban.com

NEDERLAND
* STICHTING PROSVETA NEDERLAND – 3871 TD Hoevelaken
Tel. (31) 33 25 345 75 – Fax. (31) 33 25 803 20
vermeulen@prosveta.nl – www.prosveta.nl

NORWAY
* PROSVETA Norden – N-1502 Moss – Tel. (47) 90 27 43 33 – Fax (47) 69 20 67 60
info@prosveta.no – www.prosveta.no

UNITED STATES
** Prosveta Books – Tel. (516) 674 4428
fbu_usa@hotmail.com – www.www.prosvetabooks.com
** PROSVETA US Dist. – Canyon Country CA 91387 – Tel. (661) 252-9090
usa@prosveta.com / prosveta-usa@earthlink.net – www.prosveta-usa.com

Printed in August 2018
by PRINTCORP

Dépôt légal : Août 2018